**New Directions for
Student Services**

John H. Schuh
EDITOR-IN-CHIEF

Elizabeth J. Whitt
ASSOCIATE EDITOR

Student Affairs Budgeting and Financial Management in the Midst of Fiscal Crisis

Lori E. Varlotta
Barbara C. Jones
EDITORS

Number 129 • Spring 2010
Jossey-Bass
San Francisco

STUDENT AFFAIRS BUDGETING AND FINANCIAL MANAGEMENT IN THE
MIDST OF FISCAL CRISIS
Lori E. Varlotta, Barbara C. Jones (eds.)
New Directions for Student Services, no. 129
John H. Schuh, Editor-in-Chief
Elizabeth J. Whitt, Associate Editor

NEW DIRECTIONS FOR STUDENT SERVICES (ISSN 0164-7970, e-ISSN 1536-
0695) is part of The Jossey-Bass Higher and Adult Education Series and
is published quarterly by Wiley Subscription Services, Inc., A Wiley Company, at Jossey-Bass, 989 Market Street, San Francisco, California 94103-
1741. Periodicals Postage Paid at San Francisco, California, and at
additional mailing offices. POSTMASTER: Send address changes to New
Directions for Student Services, Jossey-Bass, 989 Market Street, San Francisco, CA 94103-1741.

NEW DIRECTIONS FOR STUDENT SERVICES is indexed in CIJE: Current
Index to Journals in Education, Contents Pages in Education (T&F),
Current Abstracts (EBSCO), Education Index/Abstracts (H.W. Wilson),
Educational Research Abstracts Online (T&F), ERIC Database (Educa-
tion Resources Information Center), and Higher Education Abstracts
(Claremont Graduate University).

Microfilm copies of issues and articles are available in 16mm and 35mm,
as well as microfiche in 105mm, through University Microfilms Inc., 300
North Zeeb Road, Ann Arbor, Michigan 48106-1346.

SUBSCRIPTIONS cost $98 for individuals and $267 for institutions, agencies,
and libraries in the United States.

EDITORIAL CORRESPONDENCE should be sent to the Editor-in-Chief, John
H. Schuh, N. 243 Lagomarcino Hall, Iowa State University, Ames, Iowa
50011.

www.josseybass.com

Contents

EDITORS' NOTES

The national financial crisis that began in 2008 has forced many American colleges and universities to reduce or restructure budgets, and some economic analysts are projecting continuing difficulties for higher education. Accordingly, many higher education administrators have begun to prepare themselves for the ongoing budget reductions that are likely to result from falling state support, withdrawal of stimulus money, and volatile endowments. The pressures on higher education are great. There are those, like President Obama, who believe the economic well-being of the country rests at least in part on the success of higher education to produce graduates who will lead the country in innovative ways to a brighter future. However, with the uncertain financial future of higher education, achieving success seems much more challenging.

Campuses across the country have turned to many strategies to meet the financial challenges. In addressing the reductions, some have invoked a comprehensive strategic budget plan to inform the difficult choices and trade-offs they face. On other campuses, the cuts have been doled out as an across-the-board, or nearly across-the-board, percentage reduction. In many of these latter cases, noninstructional areas take the biggest (often uniform) hits, while instructional activities are held harmless or nearly harmless. To assist senior student affairs officers (SSAOs) and other student affairs colleagues in helping their campus make deliberate and strategic rather than quick or superficially formulaic cuts, this volume offers conceptual models, best practices, tried-and-true strategies, professional recommendations, and highlights of national trends on various issues related to budget planning, processes, communication, and alternative funding sources. It also explores the impact that continuing budget reductions have through the eyes of SSAOs who face these daily.

Toward that end, this New Directions for Student Services volume offers macrolevel summaries and analyses of budget cycles, models, and strategic communications. In Chapter One, Lori Varlotta sets the context by examining the real and potential link between planning and budgeting. In doing so, she describes both commonplace and less commonly used (but viable) models for collegiate budgeting. No matter which model and corollary strategies are employed on one's campus, she urges the SSAO to take a leadership role in the institution's overall budgeting process. Particularly in these trying times, it is crucial that the budget process and the foundational assumptions on which it is designed are shared with the

WILEY InterScience®
DISCOVER SOMETHING GREAT

NEW DIRECTIONS FOR STUDENT SERVICES, no. 129, Spring 2010 © Wiley Periodicals, Inc.
Published online in Wiley InterScience (www.interscience.wiley.com) • DOI: 10.1002/ss.346

campus community in a timely, accurate, and easy-to-understand way. Chapter Two looks at the similarities and differences of funding and budgeting between public institutions and small, private institutions. Eugene Zdziarski describes the challenges smaller colleges face in developing budget models and the impact of the current economic conditions on those models. In so doing, he provides an insightful view of the small, private college.

To drive home that point, Kurt Keppler explores revenue opportunities and cost-savings strategies in Chapter Three. He categorizes these strategies according to the decision-making entities that are involved in each and explains why particular approaches are well suited to individual institutions. Jonathan Eldridge and Tisa Mason in Chapter Four provide a comprehensive look at issues surrounding budget communications. Although the communication strategies they delineate are suitable to any budget situation, they are especially useful during economic downturns as entire academic communities are interested in both the big picture and the details of how it will affect them. Even in these difficult times, SSAOs and other student affairs leaders can be—indeed, should be—creative.

The next two chapters explore the realities of budget reduction. Chapter Five, by Renee Romano, Jan Hanish, Calvin Phillips, and Michael Waggoner, takes a multicampus look at these realities. This chapter shares the experiences of twelve SSAOs who have managed significant budget reductions at their respective public universities over the past several years. The authors review a qualitative study conducted in 2005 and 2009 and summarize pertinent excerpts from the SSAOs at the institutions studied, highlighting key trends that emerged during their interviews with these leaders and comparing similarities and differences in the responses to the budget reductions between the two surveys. Using a narrative approach, Frank Ardaiolo describes in Chapter Six the realities he faced on a single campus. In this case, he recounts the journey his campus traveled as it moved through the uncharted waters of staggering state budget cuts.

The final chapter, by Lori Varlotta, Barb Jones, and John Schuh, summarizes the three content areas explored throughout this volume, highlighting some of the key points related to budget models, communication strategies, and relationships.

We know that readers of this volume will have personal and professional experiences that are unique to the budget issues playing out on their home campuses. We also acknowledge that differences in leadership style, strategic planning, and funding models shape, if not dictate, the approach institutions draw on to resolve their budget challenges and shortfalls. Still, we hope that student affairs colleagues at all levels of institutions will be able to find nuggets within these pages as they engage fully in institution-wide budget processes. The SSAOs and divisions of student affairs can and should be significant contributors to setting the future direction of their colleges and universities by engaging fully in the process of addressing the budget crisis.

We end by expressing our sincere gratitude to Alan Haslam for his invaluable assistance in editing this volume.

Lori E. Varlotta
Barbara C. Jones
Editors

LORI E. VARLOTTA *is vice president of student affairs at California State University, Sacramento.*

BARBARA C. JONES *is vice president of student affairs at Miami University in Oxford, Ohio.*

NEW DIRECTIONS FOR STUDENT SERVICES • DOI: 10.1002/ss

1

This chapter presents information to help senior student affairs officers first establish themselves as experts in division-level budgeting and then go on to become leaders in university-wide budgeting.

Becoming a Leader in University Budgeting

Lori E. Varlotta

This chapter explains what senior student affairs officers (SSAOs) and those aspiring to the position should know and do in terms of budgeting to make the transition from division to university leadership. Before SSAOs can help lead any university-wide budget process, particularly ones that unfold amid fiscal decline, they must master divisional practices as a foundation. Toward that end, this chapter first reviews the steps that managing and aspiring SSAOs should consider when preparing divisional budgets: initiating and maintaining a meaningful strategic planning process, knowing intimately each of the budgets that constitute their overall portfolio, and meticulously responding to and involving others in the budget call or exercise.

Once they have their own shop in shape, successful SSAOs move beyond division-level budgeting to hone their macrolevel strategic and operational planning skills. These skills, reviewed next, include developing a refined understanding of the various roles of the university budget and both designing and marshaling data-driven supporting materials to actualize those roles.

In addition to examining the potential functions of the budget, budget-savvy SSAOs must study viable budget models. Hence, this chapter ends by reviewing and then delineating the advantages and challenges associated with four budget models—incremental and decremental, zero based, responsibility centered, and initiative based—commonly used in institutions of higher learning.

NEW DIRECTIONS FOR STUDENT SERVICES, no. 129, Spring 2010   © Wiley Periodicals, Inc.
Published online in Wiley InterScience (www.interscience.wiley.com) • DOI: 10.1002/ss.347

Conceptualizing and Implementing a Divisional Process

Before an SSAO can serve as a leader of the university's budget process, she must be, and be perceived as, expert in divisional budgeting. Therefore, this chapter begins with a review of the fundamental practices that help SSAOs develop budget competencies at the divisional level: implementing a divisional strategic plan that manifests the institution's mission, knowing thoroughly all divisional budgets, and responding fastidiously to the budget call or budget exercise.

Using the University's Strategic Priorities to Shape Divisional Plans. In well-managed institutions that implement best practices, the budget serves as the quantitative representation of the university's strategic plan. It is vital for SSAOs who serve in such institutions to play a central role in conceptualizing and implementing the university's strategic plan and to use that plan as the cornerstone for divisional documents that highlight mission, vision, and values. If the budget truly serves as the financial representation of the strategic plan, then resources will follow the plan's priorities in both prosperous times and tight years alike. When SSAOs map those priorities in specific and concrete ways back to the division, they almost guarantee their departments some financial support.

Before deploying a budget process built on a university's particular mission, vision, and values, however, SSAOs must understand the conception of academic strategic planning on their home campus. Some define it as an ongoing process of relevant and effective adaptation to environmental change (Meyerson and Johnson, 1993; Peterson, 1999). Others (Rowley, Lujan, and Dolence, 1997; Schuh, 2003) conceive strategic planning as the optimal alignment between an institution's programs and structures and the key components of its internal and external environment. Regardless of the exact definition an institution employs, a comprehensive strategic planning process typically includes a preplanning stage, an environmental scan and prioritization phase, an implementation plan, and an evaluation process, and effective SSAOs are involved in each phase.

During preplanning, the SSAO should work with those charged with strategic planning to revisit broadly the university's mission, vision, and values statements and any related governing documents. During this stage, the SSAO should solicit feedback from her division regarding the current renditions of these statements. Do these guiding documents, for example, put students at the center of the university? If not, should the division make note of this and recommend future revisions? The SSAO should share appropriate recommendations with those who are crafting or revising the university mission, vision, and values—all of which subsequently frame the divisional documents that guide the work of student affairs.

NEW DIRECTIONS FOR STUDENT SERVICES • DOI: 10.1002/ss

The next stage of the strategic planning process often includes a SWOT analysis—one that identifies the institution's Strengths, Weaknesses, Opportunities, and Threats—or another type of environmental scan. The purpose of the SWOT analysis is to produce a short list of priorities that the university will tackle during the next three to five years. Some of the emerging priorities should capitalize on the university's current strengths and opportunities; others should confront the existing or anticipated threats and weaknesses that make the university vulnerable. Like the mission, vision, and values statements drafted in the preplanning stage, both the summary of the SWOT analysis and its corollary priorities should be shared with campus constituents. The SSAO is one of many managers who can appropriately facilitate this dissemination.

After the priorities have been formulated and circulated around campus, the planning team (possibly in conjunction with a broader group of university members) must develop action plans that address the priorities and benchmarks that chart the university's progress in reaching them. The SSAO's input at this stage will direct the future work of the campus and the division. Many who write about strategic planning suggest that action plans be developed at the unit or departmental level (Woodard and von Destinon, 2000; Meyerson and Johnson, 1993). However, although this type of vertical planning may be a necessary part of the implementation process, it is by no means sufficient. Departmental plans must be augmented by cross-divisional ones to fully address the multifaceted and complex priorities that surface from SWOT analyses. Cross-divisional plans may be conceived as horizontal ones that draw from, depend on, and connect to various units across campus. Since most SSAOs represent numerous constituents and are often perceived as engaged campus citizens, they may be particularly effective at facilitating horizontal planning. Once departmental and cross-divisional action and assessment plans are developed and data are collected, then evaluation, the final stage of strategic planning, begins.

During the evaluation phase, campus leaders assess the extent to which the implementation plans have been realized. This assessment can be measured in part by clarifying whether outcomes formulated during the previous stage have been achieved and whether predetermined benchmarks (or other types of measurable targets that go by any number of names) have been met. Progress and shortfalls alike must be communicated clearly to the campus community, and there should be little shame or defensiveness in not meeting every goal. Respectable benchmarks, after all, are set as stretch goals rather than as easy-to-hit targets. Well-designed and practical assessment is an iterative process that uses data-driven feedback and analysis to modify and improve programs and services. Like the assessment process itself, these stages of the strategic planning process flow into each other, inform each other, and constantly evolve with the SSAO's input and attention.

Ideally SSAOs will secure a seat at each stage. Early in the strategic planning process, this seat gives firsthand knowledge of the priorities that emerge from SWOT, allowing them to be aware of the context from which the priorities and benchmarks emerged. Being privy to inside conversations clarifies priorities in ways that go beyond merely reading their final iterations. The resulting clarification allows SSAOs not only to incorporate priorities explicitly into their divisional plans, but to address the nuances that may not be apparent to less-informed leaders. If a certain division subsequently demonstrates that it contributed to helping the university meet these priorities, then that division should be recognized in the budget decision process.

Since many campuses try to hold instructional activities harmless during budget crises, it is important that student affairs proactively make transparent the many connections that tie their own programs and services to the academic mission and priorities of the university. Otherwise student affairs may be vulnerable to disproportionately high cuts during budget recessions. The following point, then, deserves highlighting: the strategic plan should always be in operation since informed decision making never ceases, even amid a budget crisis. Indeed, a full-blown fiscal crisis may prompt an institution to curtail some of the action plans associated with meeting priorities. Still, whatever priorities are ultimately addressed during tough times should map directly back to those delineated in the strategic plan. To recap an important point that is often set aside and replaced by reactionary measures on far too many campuses, even in a looming or existing budget crisis, well-managed institutions neither abandon their strategic plans to idle in some sort of immediate resting place nor create a new or distinct list of strategic priorities to direct the pressing reductions that are likely to occur. A deliberate adherence to mission, goals, and priorities will likely provide university members with a sense of reassurance and steadiness amid trying and unstable times.

Comprehending Departmental Budgets. Just as SSAOs must have skillful knowledge of how the university's priorities shape divisional action plans, so must they have a thorough understanding of how those priorities are reflected in the multiple budgets that constitute their overall portfolio. While seasoned SSAOs understand the different types of budgets they manage, those aspiring to the position may benefit from the following overview that summarizes the types of budgets that typically constitute the total student affairs portfolio.

Operating Budgets. In most cases, the division's core budgets are known as the operating budgets. In each department, these budgets reflect all of the revenues and allocations received and all of the expenses incurred during a single academic year. Salary lines reflect the largest item in any college or university's operating budget (they hover around 75 to 80 percent; Goldstein, 2005). In some academic institutions, particularly private colleges, salaries may be teased out as a stand-alone line. In addition, the operating budget may be tapped for equipment, supplies, telecommunication, staff training, and travel. At some colleges and universities, this is the budget that also covers certain cost allocations such as utilities or charge backs for internal services (like technology, campus police, and maintenance upgrades) that the unit is expected to finance. In public universities, departmental operating budgets typically are supported by the general fund. The general fund is allocated by the state legislature to its state colleges and universities, often in accordance with some type of full-time equivalency (FTE) formula or per student subsidy. Other funds that may support the operating budgets of public and private colleges alike are student fees, endowments and gifts, grants, and sponsored programs.

Auxiliary Budgets. Student affairs' auxiliary budgets, which can easily account for more than 80 percent of an SSAO's budget portfolio (Woodard, Love, and Komives, 2000), reflect the revenues generated and the expenses incurred from enterprises such as residential life and housing, the student union, health centers, the bookstore, and food services. The revenues generated through auxiliary units not only support the expenses mentioned above (salary and operational) but all of the expenses incurred by the enterprise, including those that come from debt service, utilities, and infrastructure. In most institutions, public and private, auxiliary budgets are segregated from the general fund budget or the overall educational budget since the units they support are intended to operate without any subsidy from the institution (Schuh, 2003). Conversely, the revenues that auxiliaries generate are used to subsidize the institution's mission (Schuh citing Lennington, 2003).

Capital Budgets. In addition to managing operating and auxiliary budgets, many SSAOs also oversee the capital budgets that support the construction of new student facilities such as residence halls and recreation centers, the acquisition of property such as nearby apartments, or the major renovations of existing structures. In many cases, the capital budget includes borrowed funds that come in the form of construction loans or long-term bonds. A construction loan is usually a short-term one (often three years) that is meant to cover the land development and building construction costs of a property being financed. A long-term bond finances the purchase or construction costs of new facilities, including its major equipment and infrastructure; long-term bonds are to the university what a home mortgage is to an individual home owner (Goldstein, 2005).

The Reserve. To add another dimension to the three aforementioned budgets that SSAOs typically oversee, SSAOs who are permitted to carry over unexpended resources from one year to the next also manage another type of budget, the reserve. As the name suggests, reserves are the savings amassed and maintained when a department does not spend its entire initial allocation. On some campuses, the SSAO has jurisdiction to use the reserves at any point to support items that are at her discretion. At other institutions, she is expected to use the reserve within a particular timeframe to finance predetermined priorities.

To become entirely familiar with all of the budgets that constitute the whole, an SSAO, particularly one new to the position, must learn the policies and practices associated with each type of budget she oversees for her individual institution. No two universities handle budgeting exactly alike. On some campuses, funds from various types of budgets can be commingled, while on others, this practice is explicitly prohibited. The ways that monies are accessed and expended within a single type of budget also vary significantly from institution to institution. At some universities, the budget is organized by unique and impermeable line items. In contrast, other universities may allow frequent movement between budget lines as long as the bottom line is balanced.

The important point is that SSAOs must learn, as early in their tenure as possible, the policies, practices, and idiosyncrasies that govern budget processes at their institution. Fully grasping these nuances takes time and effort, neither of which is readily available during a budget crisis. On campuses facing budget crises, many SSAOs are forced to operate primarily in a reactive mode as they address budget edicts and rework reduction scenarios to align with the projections that are often changing. Therefore, the chances of an SSAO being able to make any creative or proactive budget decisions amid an economic downturn increase dramatically if she has honed her understanding of divisional budgets, their intended uses, funding sources, and peculiarities long before the crisis hits.

Responding to the Budget Call. At certain points in any academic year, the SSAO likely is involved in three distinct budget cycles concurrently: closing out the previous fiscal year, monitoring current year balances, and projecting revenue and expenses for the upcoming one (Barr, 2002). This makes the final step in divisional budgeting—knowing, in depth, the entire budget process (budget guidelines, cycles, underlying assumptions, possibilities for alternatives or troubleshooting, and deadlines for submission)—critically important. The most viable way for an SSAO to approach this step is to see her actions as being both proactive and reactive.

Clearly part of the SSAO's response to the budget call or exercise will be reactive: noting and adhering to guidelines, following precisely the directions of the call, completing budget forms accurately, and submitting final documents on or before deadlines. Accuracy, precision, and timeliness of budget materials are of utmost importance during budget reductions when reviewers must weigh competing yet important interests against each other.

It is essential, however, that the SSAO do more than respond to the call. In terms of being proactive in divisional budgeting, the SSAO must gather unit-level information from as many staff as appropriate, organize that information according to the budget instructions, disseminate the emerging draft back to staff, identify challenges, forecast problems, develop alternatives based on feedback, and submit, on time, all final documents, while keeping staff informed throughout the entire process. Managing all of these aspects of the budget cycle simultaneously may seem daunting, but once SSAOs

NEW DIRECTIONS FOR STUDENT SERVICES • DOI: 10.1002/ss

become accustomed to the fluid give-and-take of communication, analyses, and action, the process becomes a manageable part of everyday duties.

Throughout the university, the budget process itself is as important as the final product. This is particularly true in student affairs, a division that characteristically attracts people-oriented staff who confer, consult, and deliberate together. The timely dissemination of budget assumptions, projections, and decisions is always important; it is especially crucial in troubled times when rumor mills and imaginations can conjure up notions that are far worse than what is in fact approaching. (Chapter Five on budget communications addresses this point and related ones in great detail.)

Understanding and Maximizing the Roles of the Campus Budget

In highly functioning universities that follow best practices, the budget assumes and noticeably performs three vital roles: supporting the strategic plan, illustrating how money follows mission; clarifying organizational work agreements between supervisors and their staff; and reflecting the trade-offs that have been made as part of the budget process. For any number of reasons, however, these roles are not fully enacted on many campuses. To help SSAOs execute these roles and meet the expectations associated with them, we examine the theoretical role being discussed and present a concrete mechanism that can help bring that particular function to fruition.

Supporting the Strategic Plan. The budget's preeminent role is to serve as the quantitative representation of the university's strategic plan. The budget unequivocally reveals to all invested parties where the institution is spending its resources, which subsequently highlights the paramount goals of the campus leadership team (Barr, 2002). In well-organized universities, the overlap between where the university is putting its financial resources, and what the strategic plan has highlighted as it prioritizes, is precise. In these institutions, the budget is not a loose representation but rather an actual "blueprint of what is important" (Barr, 2002, p. 30). On these campuses, the budget unambiguously substantiates that the university is putting its money where its mouth (or mission) is.

One way for SSAOs to emphasize the overlap between budgeting and planning is to create easy-to-read planning and assessment reports. These reports may be included in the divisional budget materials that SSAOs submit to the university president or university budget office. The reports should highlight the concrete strategies that are initiated and monitored by student affairs units in their ongoing quest to actualize university goals and address university priorities. There is no one way to write the reports, but the template designed by student affairs directors at California State University, Sacramento has worked well in terms of both departmental monitoring and securing additional resources during the university-wide budget process. (The reports can be downloaded from http://saweb.csus.edu/students/assessment.aspx.)

Organizing and Supporting Appropriate Workloads. Another potential role of the university's budget is to serve as an agreement of sorts among managers, their units, and their staff. In this sense, the budget has the capacity to be more than a quantitative instrument that metes out resources to departments and units; theoretically and practically, it can serve as an organizational catalyst that prompts managers and staff to work efficiently and effectively. To actualize the organizational role of the budget, SSAOs might consider using three budget-related strategies: workload estimators, cost savings, and activity-based costing.

Workload Estimators. Workload estimators are devices that measure both the "scope and magnitude of a service or program and who is served and benefited by these functions" (Woodard and von Destinon, 2000, p. 339). For example, in student affairs, workload estimators can be used to reflect how long it reasonably takes to complete a unique activity (reviewing an admission application, perhaps). This estimated time spent on each activity (in this case, thirty minutes of review time per application) is then multiplied by the total number of assignments that need to be completed during the specific time period (in this example, the overall number of admission applications that need to be evaluated during the priority filing months). This resulting product by and large reveals to managers how many staff hours are needed to assess applications and to make acceptance and denial decisions. The total staff hours can then be used to predict how many admission counselors will be needed, during the time frame allotted, to review the total number of applications received.

Workload estimators are useful evaluative tools in any budgeting cycle and can be especially crucial during tough cycles when allocations are likely to be reduced. In lean times, workload estimators can be used to corroborate the need for maintaining or increasing current staffing levels. During difficult budget cycles, many institutions protect instructional activity in ways that prompt disproportionate cuts to other areas. If such cuts are projected to hit key service areas like admissions, financial aid, the registrar's office, and the advising center—all of whose work is somewhat quantifiable in terms of time needed to serve projected users—then SSAOs can design workload estimators to verify the number of staff needed to complete essential assignments.

Cost Savings. Cost savings is another fairly straightforward strategy that SSAOs can use to maximize the organizational role of the budget. In terms of cost savings measures, SSAOs might propose various forms of cross-departmental training, possible outsourcing, unit mergers, consolidation of positions, keeping vacancies open, or the reductions of duplicative or similar services. However, overall divisional savings cannot be realized unless an integrative reduction plan is in place. In other words, real savings do not accrue if one unit is expected to absorb the reductions of another. (Chapter

NEW DIRECTIONS FOR STUDENT SERVICES • DOI: 10.1002/ss

Four examines how real savings accrue through mergers, outsourcing, and position shifting.)

Activity-Based Costing. Activity-based costing (ABC) is a specific cost-control mechanism that can add nuance to and maximize workload estimators and other cost savings strategies. The goal is to formulate reliable and usable cost information that genuinely reflects the "cause and effect relationships between costs, activities and products or services" (Hicks, 1999, p. 5). While ABC and other forms of cost accountability are frequently included in the everyday work of American business professionals and the budgets they design, they have been infrequently discussed and rarely incorporated into collegiate budget calls or supporting budget materials. Given this reality, SSAOs and other academic leaders may need to look to corporate America for best practices in this area.

Especially in tight budget times, universities are increasingly viewed with the same scrutiny and pragmatism as businesses. Given the business world's interest in profitability, however, it is unlikely that a corporate cost control model can be universally applied to the university environs. Although complete transferability is implausible, SSAOs may nevertheless find elements of corporate cost models to be practical and constructive.

The ABC model has elicited much corporate attention (both positive and negative) in the past decade or so. Its goal is to map and render transparent the often complex web of cause-and-effect relationships among costs, activities, and products or services. Once those are well understood, ABC creates concrete, evidence-based cost information regarding those relationships. Unlike traditional accounting, which focuses primarily on the calculation of the indirect costs of a company's overhead (utilities, marketing, distribution), ABC also considers the time that professionals spend on developing and producing a product or delivering a service ("Activity-Based Costing," 2009). This attempt to quantify the relationship between cost and time may be of great interest to academic leaders who wish to create workload estimators in areas that do not easily lend themselves to such quantifications.

It was easy to estimate, in the example above, how long it takes to review an admissions application. But how long does it take—and how long should it take—to develop a semester-long cocurricular leadership program? Does the ABC model indicate how a manager can account for, or validate this type of time spent on a task? In other words, does this model (or any other model) capture more than how much time is spent? Can it measure how well the time is spent and who exactly is expending it? SSAOs and other managers who are interested in considering these questions may find Kaplan and Anderson's *Time-Driven Activity Based Costing* (2007) a starting point.

Reflecting the Primary Trade-Offs. Hypothetically, another key function of the budget is to illuminate the trade-offs made during the process by chief stakeholders. In practice, however, these negotiations become embedded, making it difficult for those not directly involved to see or understand how underlying decisions were made. Although trade-offs occur in every budget cycle, they are likely to increase in both number and substance when resources are scarce. To make transparent the trade-offs that are in play especially in precarious times, SSAOs might consider using a trade-off model that clarifies and systemically delineates how decisions were made.

Blomquist, Newsome, and Stone (2009) have designed such a model. They describe a contingent budget allocation technique that increases citizen participation in budgeting by prompting them to trade off one public program for enhancements to another given the specified budget. This thought-provoking article may help SSAOs articulate the types of choices and trade-offs embedded in campus budgets.

There is no doubt that the budget's trade-off role is a highly political one that involves ongoing compromises. To maximize this role and garner positive benefits from it, the trade-offs—to the largest extent possible—should be overt and the discussions that help formulate them should be inclusive. Wildavsky puts it well in a statement that comments on both trade-offs and budgeting at large: "If politics is regarded as conflict over whose preferences are to prevail in the determination of policy, then the budget records the outcomes of this struggle" (Layzell and Lyddon, 1996, p. 319). Indeed, the university budget at all levels reflects the priorities and preferences that "win" year to year. Effective SSAOs can do their part to ensure that the values the budget represents in dollar signs mirror the campus values that have been formulated, circulated, and endorsed.

Knowing About and Becoming Conversant in Budget Approaches

As SSAOs move from division to university-wide budgeting, they must not be very familiar only with the budget models currently used on their campus, but must become aware as well of other approaches that may complement or replace the ones routinely used. An understanding of complementary or alternative models is profoundly beneficial in nonroutine budget situations. During a dire budget cycle, for example, it may be wise for leaders to use a budget model that differs drastically from the one used in stable years when there is little change in revenues or expenses. Just as distinctively different situations (such as a strategic planning meeting, a year-end managerial retreat, a brawl at a home football game, or an active shooter emergency) call for a specific style of leadership (the term for this is *situational leadership*), a unique budget situation requires a budget model geared to address the challenges being faced. If the leadership analogy is applied to budgeting, then SSAOs may think of this as situational budgeting.

This section outlines several approaches deployed on campuses throughout the United States, identifying which models may be used in tight times. This review and analysis will not only help SSAOs become conversant in any number or combination of feasible budget approaches but will also help them identify the models most appropriate for current conditions. Budget-savvy SSAOs realize that neither the divisional nor the overall university budget needs to adhere to a single budget approach. In both cases, the most effective budget may draw on a combination of budget approaches. Cognizant of this reality, SSAOs must become familiar with the strengths, weaknesses, and utility of each of the models described next.

Incremental and Decremental Budgeting. Incremental and decremental budgeting makes incremental upward or downward adjustments to budget allocations, expressed as percentage increases or decreases from the previous year's budget. It is the most widely used budget approach in higher education (Schuh, 2003). With incremental budgeting, increases are consistently applied across units or line items. On some campuses where revenues are increasing, the individual allocation to each department or unit is increased by an exact percentage no matter where the unit is housed or what functions it provides. On other campuses, incremental adjustments may be applied to specific line items, for example, all salaries could be adjusted upward by the same percentage. If, conversely, the institution is in a reduction mode, the percentage cut deemed necessary by the leadership team and the business office is applied unilaterally to all units or specific line items.

The advantage of incremental and decremental budgeting is that the uniform application of increases and decreases lessens conflict and expedites decision making. On a conceptual level, this budgeting is easy to describe, and university members quickly comprehend the apparent rationale that undergirds the model. Similarly, from an implementation perspective, the model is simple to operationalize; in fact, it is virtually automatic.

Unfortunately the two foundational assumptions on which incremental and decremental budgeting rests are often flawed: that needs (including university priorities) and costs vary insignificantly from year to year and that the previous budgets have been pretty much on target. Even in situations where the assumptions are more or less accurate, the incremental and decremental approach obstructs critical examination, challenge, and inquiry. Instead it maintains the status quo and covertly perpetuates the notion that on-the-mark budgeting has been and continues to be in play. In other words, it appears fair and equitable because it seemingly treats all institutional entities and line items the same. In reality, however, each entity and line item is treated equally only in relationship to the status quo. When this approach is used, there is never any reason to reevaluate the status quo, and this can cause dual problems. For example, on a campus where a long-standing allocation no longer covers new or additional programs or services, then even an incrementally increased allocation is likely to fall short of covering current expenses. Conversely, if an established amount is allocated to a department that has recently reduced offerings or realized cost savings from new technologies, for example, the electronic dissemination of formerly hard copy, mail-delivered materials, then the actual allocation may exceed expenses.

Another major problem with incremental and decremental budgeting is that it gives no financial allowance to units that are supporting university

NEW DIRECTIONS FOR STUDENT SERVICES • DOI: 10.1002/ss

priorities since all increases are evenly doled out across the board. This means that units that are charged with or have taken the leadership role in addressing strategic priorities receive the same amounts of resources as units that have assumed none of these responsibilities.

A third problem with this method of budgeting is that it operates only at the margins (Goldstein, 2005) of an institution's budget, making small changes that prevent the types of reallocation, redistribution, or "right-sizing" that potentially benefit many divisions, particularly student affairs. This is a serious limitation for divisions like student affairs, which (according to the U.S. Department of Education) traditionally receive less than 10 percent of the institution's overall budget allocations.

In summary, the incremental and decremental approach is the most likely to maintain the status quo and the least likely to catalyze change. As such, it is not viable for helping administrators actualize their strategic plan or for facilitating the types of decisions that should be made in challenging budget years. Unfortunately, its broad application in higher education suggests that "the need for efficiency in some administrative areas outweighs the desire for effectiveness" (Goldstein, 2005, p. 165).

Zero-Based Budgeting. Zero-based budgeting (ZBB) in some ways could be perceived as the opposite of incremental budgeting. Whereas the latter presumes little change in goals or year-to-year allocations, ZBB starts from scratch each year. Using the ZBB approach, each unit revisits its goals, formulates the action plans and objectives that will help meet these goals, prioritizes the emerging objectives, proposes the types and amounts of resources needed to bring them to fruition, identifies alternate modes or methods for delivery, and justifies the final requests. The budget proposal, built anew each year, is directly correlated to the costs of implementing plans, reaching goals, and hitting benchmarks or objectives. Since ZBB does not automatically assume a given or secured funding level that supports a prescribed set of programs or services, it is a model that reconstructs each year's or cycle's budget anew. This inherent and defining feature of the ZBB model is expressly useful for directing budget processes that include deep analyses or major reallocation of resources.

If conscientiously applied in the way that ZBB is intended, this approach not only initiates a budget-planning connectivity, but it also re-examines the basic elements—goals, objectives, measures, and benchmarks—of any strategic plan. Such an examination may be timely in tight years when units are prompted to "get back to the basics" and postpone or downsize programs and services that are too costly to offer in meager times.

The process that managers and staff undertake to build a ZBB budget is a long and labor-intensive one that necessitates decision making at each step and every level. For this reason, it is not the most popular model used on campuses today. Frequently when ZBB surfaces as a possible approach for structuring the university budget process, it is conceived as a comprehensive model. As such, it can be perceived as a monumental undertaking; it need not, however, be seen as an all-or-nothing proposition (Goldstein, 2005). Constructing an entire university's (or division's) budget from ground level may be unrealistic, but it may be feasible and even productive to use the ZBB approach for a portion of the university's or division's budget (Goldstein, 2005). For example, if a new strategic plan has just been adopted, the SSAO could set aside ten percent of the division's operating budget for zero-based proposals that support the new plan. Applying the model to a designated portion of the university's overall budget would be a reasonable assignment that would likely create a valuable teaching and learning moment for all involved.

Responsibility-Centered Budgeting. Responsibility-centered budgeting is described in everyday parlance as "every boat floats on its own bottom." In professional terms, this transforms individual colleges, departments, and units of the university into "revenue centers," "cost centers," or "hybrid centers," each with full access to the direct and indirect revenues it generates in exchange for covering the expenses it incurs. As an example, the dean of each academic college is given control of the portion of tuition, fees, or state allocation it generates in enrolling its total FTE (Goldstein, 2005). In addition, the dean is given access to the extramural funds that faculty and staff within the college are awarded through grants and special programs. The dean then uses these "revenues" to fund the expenses incurred by the college. Typically a center is expected to cover its obvious expenses like salary, travel, and rental of on- and off-campus space and laboratories, along with its less-obvious charge backs. Charge backs are imposed on the center to subsidize the costs associated with internal services. In this situation, a revenue or cost center is charged its fair portion of services such as utilities, telecommunications, infrastructure costs, and facilities. The portion or charge back that each center pays is sometimes determined by mutually agreed-on formulas or state, federal, or professional association guidelines. In addition to paying for its charge backs, the center also may be "taxed" on the external money it attracts in grants and other sponsored programs (Goldstein, 2005).

The responsibility-centered approach engenders a broader understanding of university budgeting since larger numbers of administrators are compelled to recognize and manage all of the costs of doing business. Rather than rest the university's financial responsibility in the hands of a few senior administrators, it distributes it widely about the campus, encouraging internal stakeholders to be engaged and empowered. External stakeholders like parents, legislators, and community members may favor this approach as it makes visible costs that can otherwise be hidden. In the minds of stakeholders, unearthing covert costs is the first step in containing them. Since cost containment and accountability have wide appeal during economic downturns, the responsibility-centered approach may be popular during budget recessions.

Although responsibility-centered budgeting has some advantages in spreading around authority and accountability, this approach has downsides as well. Perhaps the biggest drawback is its primary focus on the bottom line. This focus potentially detracts from quality if it prompts centers to choose the most cost-effective pedagogies, class structures, or course schedules over the most educationally purposeful. Another disadvantage commonly associated with this approach is that it can foster unhealthy competition between colleges and departments—encouraging individual units to favor what is best for themselves over what is most beneficial for the entire institution. Finally, from an organizational perspective, this approach is difficult to operationalize on a large scale since many broad-based service units are not directly linked to discrete revenue streams. Therefore, while a cost- or revenue-centered model may work for some parts of the institution, it does not lend itself easily to every type of organizational unit.

Initiative-Based Budgeting. Initiative-based budgeting centrally pools for redistribution a small percentage of department or unit budgets. This set-aside fund is then earmarked for current or emerging priorities, proposed as initiatives. Campuses that use initiative-based budgeting often require an individual unit to submit a proposal that illustrates how it will use a portion of the pooled funds to directly support a specific priority or actualize an important university goal. Initiative-based budgeting is more practical in lucrative years when units can skim off a portion of their initial allocation without devastating their overall budget. If it is continued during a downturn, it is imperative that only the most strategic and time-sensitive priorities are funded. The resourcing of any superfluous initiatives will justifiably cause resentment since their support will, in effect, have come at the cost of some other program or service.

Initiative-based budgeting is not a comprehensive model. Instead, it is a short-term or midterm budget strategy, most often used in conjunction with a larger budget approach, since most units cannot indefinitely wheedle out parts of their initial allocation. On many campuses, initiative-based budgeting fuels creativity and triggers planning and budgeting integration; it allows departments that are awarded funds to respond in timely and unique ways to a contemporary issue. In good times, in particular, this can activate a stimulating process that launches an exciting new program. The sustainability of the sponsored program is questionable, however, since the support is typically allocated on a one-time rather than ongoing basis.

Other Models. This section includes only a partial list of budget approaches. Less commonly used models include planning, program, and budgeting system models that synthesize planning, operational analyses, and cost-benefit ratios to illuminate the financial implications of program decisions; formula-based models used to allocate a portion of state general funds to their state universities; and performance-based models that weigh

NEW DIRECTIONS FOR STUDENT SERVICES • DOI: 10.1002/ss

inputs against outcomes. Readers who are interested in learning more about these intermittently used approaches are referred to *College and University Budgeting: An Introduction for Faculty and Academic Administrators*, published by NACUBO and updated every few years.

Conclusion

As SSAOs enact more prominent roles in university budgeting, they master their divisional budget process, understand the roles of the campus budget and maximize them for their division and the constituents they serve, and know the methodology and utility associated with conventional budget models. It is also important for SSAOs to be able to differentiate the various models of budgeting from each other, anticipating the advantages and disadvantages of each. In addition, it is even more critical that SSAOs understand thoroughly how their campus models are chosen and retained. They must be able to discern the extent to which the budget models themselves, their underlying purposes, and the various roles the budget assumes can be questioned, challenged, or changed.

This chapter has provided SSAOs with conceptual models and concrete strategies that should be carefully considered, tested, and used as appropriate. On most campuses, successful changes to university budget models and practices come incrementally, step-by-step, rather than in one fell swoop. Budget-proficient SSAOs will work with others to identify what is working in regard to their comprehensive campus budget, preserving the functional bits and pieces as a means to improving the future. They will not impulsively supplant established models or strategies with new ones that sounded impressive at a conference or read well in a journal article.

Although this chapter has described various budget processes, components, functions, and models, the budget is more than the sum of its parts. It is as much a management and leadership tool as it is a quantitative or computational exercise (Finney, 1994). But even more than being a leadership device, the budget is a leadership conveyance. As a tool, the budget is sharpened by the talents that effective SSAOs use in every other aspect of their work: planning, projecting, organizing, sharing, and selling. As SSAOs become experts in university budgeting, the budget morphs from an unpleasant chore to becoming a tool that facilitates their work and works for them. And the more the budget works for SSAOs, the more likely it is to work for the university members who matter most: the students. As a conveyance, the budget expresses the type of leadership embodied in those who have designed it. In this very weighty sense, SSAOs can use the budget as a mirror to reflect the type of leader they have become. By applying the information contained in this chapter to the parts of their budgets that can potentially benefit, SSAOs may like the image they see in that budget mirror.

References

"Activity-Based Costing." *Economist*, June 29, 2009. Retrieved July 3, 2009, from http://www.economist.com.

Barr, M. J. *Academic Administrator's Guide to Budgets and Financial Management*. San Francisco: Jossey-Bass, 2002.

Blomquist, G. C., Newsome, M. A., and Stone, D. B. "Public Preferences for Program Tradeoffs: Community Values for Budget Priorities." Retrieved July 1, 2009, from http://gatton.uky.edu/faculty/blomquist/ForthPBF11403.pdf.

"Expenditures of Public Degree-Grant Institutions, by Purpose of Expenditure and Type of Institution: 2003–04, 2004–05, and 2005–06." Retrieved July 2, 2009, from http://nces.ed.gov/programs/digest/d08/tables/dt08_362.asp.

Finney, R. G. *Basics of Budgeting*. New York: AMACOM, 1994.

Goldstein, L. *College and University Budgeting: An Introduction for Faculty and Academic Administrators*. Washington, D.C.: NACUBO, 2005.

Hicks, D. T. *Activity-Based Costing: Making it Work for Small and Mid-Sized Companies*. (2nd ed.) New York: Wiley, 1999.

Kaplan, R. S., & Anderson, S. *Time-Driven Activity Based Costing*. Boston: Harvard Business School Press, 2007.

Layzell, D.T., & Lyddon, J.W. "Budgeting for Higher Education at the State Level: Enigma, Paradox, and Ritual." In D.W. Breneman, L.L. Leslie & R.E. Anderson (eds.), *ASHE Reader on Finance in Higher Education*. Needham Heights, MA; Simon & Schuster, 1996.

Meyerson, J. W., & Johnson, S. L. "Planning for Strategic Decision Making." In R. T. Ingram & Associates (Eds.), *Governing Public Colleges and Universities: A Handbook for Trustees, Chief Executives, and Other Campus Leaders*. San Francisco: Jossey-Bass, 1993.

NACUBO. *Explaining College Costs*. Washington, D.C.: NACUBO, 2002.

Peterson, M. W. "Analyzing Alternative Approaches to Planning." In M. W. Peterson (ed.), *ASHE Reader on Planning and Institutional Research*. Needham Heights: Allyn & Bacon, 1999.

Rowley, D. J., Lujan, H. D., and Dolence, M. G. *Strategic Change in Colleges and Universities: Planning to Survive and Prosper*. San Francisco: Jossey-Bass, 1997.

Schuh, J. H. "Strategic Planning and Finance." In D. B. Woodard Jr. and S. R. Komives (eds.), *Student Services: A Handbook for the Profession* (4th ed.). Jossey-Bass, 2003.

Woodard, D. B., Jr., Love, P., & Komives, S. R. (eds.). *Leadership and Management Issues for a New Century*. New Directions for Student Services, no. 92. San Francisco: Jossey-Bass, 2000.

Woodard, D. B., Jr. & von Destinon, M. "Budgeting and Fiscal Management." In M. J. Barr, M. K. Desler, and Associates (eds.), *The Handbook of Student Affairs Administration* (2nd ed.). San Francisco: Jossey-Bass, 2000.

LORI E. VARLOTTA is the vice president of student affairs at California State University, Sacramento.

2

Some significant differences exist in institutional budgeting and financing between large universities and small colleges. This chapter looks at these differences and describes some of the issues senior student affairs officers need to become familiar with in order to take on a leadership role in the stewardship of their institution.

A Small College Perspective on Institutional Budget Issues

Eugene L. Zdziarski II

Chapter One presented information on divisional and university-wide budgeting processes to assist senior student affairs officers in being and becoming budget leaders within their institution. Although this information is applicable to all institutions, small and large, there are nuances and differences between large universities and small colleges in their approaches to budgeting and financing the institution. This chapter explores some of those differences and the impact it has on student affairs and the institutional budgeting process.

I am by no means an expert on higher education finance, nor do I attempt to speak for all small colleges. As a student affairs professional for more than twenty years, I have spent most of my career in large public institutions and only recently have made a transition to a small private college. Therefore, this chapter presents my personal observations and reflections on some of the key differences in institutional budgeting and finance.

Tuition

Perhaps the most conspicuous difference I have observed between large public institutions and small private colleges is in how tuition is set. Tuition is the lifeblood of virtually any institution's budget. In concept, it should reflect the actual cost to provide a student an education at a particular institution, yet any link between tuition and the cost of providing a student an education at a public institution is tenuous at best.

NEW DIRECTIONS FOR STUDENT SERVICES, no. 129, Spring 2010 © Wiley Periodicals, Inc.
Published online in Wiley InterScience (www.interscience.wiley.com) • DOI: 10.1002/ss.348

In a large public institution, out-of-state tuition is often considered an accurate reflection of the true cost of providing a student an education. In-state tuition is then the out-of-state tuition less the state contribution to a resident student's education. In concept, this logic makes a lot of sense; however, with growing public concern regarding the rising costs of higher education and the demands education has placed on many state budgets, many state legislatures now regulate tuition for state institutions. Tuition rates are set by a political process that appears to have little connection to the costs of providing that education; this process is well outside the scope of the institution and its cabinet and instead depends on the projections of state revenues and the agendas of the state legislators. As a result, administrators at public institutions can sometimes feel powerless in leading and guiding the institution and its financial future, at least in terms of tuition levels.

Conversely there is almost a sense of empowerment at private institutions during the budgeting process. Tuition is more closely tied to the true cost of providing a student an education at that particular institution and is often meticulously calculated and analyzed. Although the actual fee is ultimately approved by the board of trustees, the cabinet members work together to articulate costs, develop revenue projections, identify risks, and put together a tuition recommendation for the president to take to the board. This is not to say that everything is rosy in the institutional budgeting process and everyone gets what they want. Much work, intense debate, and difficult decisions characterize the process, but in the end, there is often a greater sense of institutional control and ability to lead an institution to fulfill its mission and strategic vision.

To participate fully in the institutional budgeting process, a senior student affairs officer (SSAO) needs to be well versed in not only her functional areas but have a solid understanding of operations in the other divisions as well. She needs to understand yields, auxiliary margins, bond rates, market indexes, and myriad other financial terms and concepts to which she may not have been previously exposed. SSAOs should consult with their chief business affairs officer or other appropriate individuals and seek additional information on the topics and aspects of the financial picture unfamiliar to them. Most of all, SSAOs should not be afraid to ask questions; in a group discussion, as in a classroom, the person asking the question is likely not the only one who is unclear. Often the team as a whole benefits from a periodic refresher on the topic.

Discount Rate

Another key difference in budgets of large public institutions and smaller private institutions is the concept of the discount rate: the portion of institutional funds used to offset the cost of a student's education based on financial need. Essentially it is a form of institutional financial aid. Much like enrollment projections, an institution attempts to project the discount rate for the coming fiscal year. The lower the discount rate, the more revenue it has to fund other priorities.

Although the concept of discount rate is most closely associated with private institutions, it is not entirely foreign to public universities. Some public institutions charge a financial aid fee (University of Florida, 2009) as part of overall tuition and fees, and then use the funds collected to provide financial assistance to students with unmet need.

In private institutions, students with unmet need are charged a lower amount of tuition or their tuition is discounted. Instead of a separate fee, this discount rate is factored into the overall institutional tuition calculation, and in the end, some students pay a higher portion of tuition, which funds the balance of students charged a lower tuition.

As higher education costs have risen over the years, so too has the discount rate, which has averaged approximately 35 percent (Krause, 2009). With the recent economic downturn, college presidents are reporting that they are offering even larger discounts (Stripling, 2009).

Obviously the strategy in the budgeting process is to hold down this discount rate as much as possible. To do so, the institution must attract and enroll students with a greater ability to pay a larger portion of the full cost of tuition.

Institutional efforts to lower the discount rate present two significant concerns for SSAOs. First, in the effort to hold down the discount rate, institutions recruit students from higher socioeconomic status, which can have a significant impact on the diversity of the campus. As institutions struggle to address the financial hurdles presented in today's economic climate, SSAOs need to champion the value of maintaining a diverse student body and the benefits it brings to the educational experience for all students.

Second, the greater the effort is to reduce the discount rate, the more likely that conflicts will arise between admissions and financial aid staff who may be facing competing priorities. While admissions staff are trying to hit their recruitment goals, financial aid staff are struggling to keep the discount rate within the prescribed range and may not be able to put together the types of aid packages that are sufficient to secure a potential student's enrollment. Because the performance of both the admissions staff and the financial aid staff may be judged by their ability to achieve these assigned goals, SSAOs may find themselves mediating between the two staffs. It is essential that both staffs have a clear understanding of the expectations placed on each office and acknowledge the inherent conflict that exists. Strong lines of communication must be established, and a balanced perspective must be maintained particularly in challenging economic times.

Enrollment Versus Endowment

Another key difference in the financing of private colleges is the delicate balance that exists between an institution's dependence on enrollment and its dependence on its endowment to fund college operations. Student enrollment provides tuition dollars that form the basis of a college budget. College administrators must formulate annual projections for both the recruitment of new students and the retention of current students. While historical data can be used to identify trends and assist in the development of these projections, significant changes in the economy bring greater uncertainty into the process. For example, with the tightening of the economy, institutions nationwide have seen a rise in the number of applications for admission; however, the yields on these applications have been lower than many institutions had projected (Hoover, 2009). Furthermore, the downturn in the economy has forced some currently enrolled students to postpone their educational goals because of financial concerns, which then affects institutional retention projections. Because of factors such as these, confidence in traditional indicators of student enrollment has wavered, and budget projections based on these indicators can be tenuous at best.

Given the uncertainty associated with budgets based on student enrollment projections, some institutions have relied more heavily on their endowments to fund their annual budget. An endowment is a collection of institutional assets (money or property) that has been donated to the institution and invested. A percentage of the endowment is withdrawn annually to supplement the institution's annual budget. Generally an institution will use approximately five percent of the endowment annually to fund institutional operating expenses, but in difficult financial times, this percentage can increase (Tharp, 2001).

In some cases, institutions have such large endowments that a significant portion of their institutional expenditures is routinely funded by their endowments. For example, Harvard University is generally considered one of the top institutions in the country and boasts the largest university endowment with over $36 billion (NACUBO, 2009). With such incredible resources on which to draw to fund institutional operations and its strong reputation, Harvard can afford to be highly selective in student admissions and be relatively unconcerned about enrollment projections. It is reported that Harvard funds approximately one third of its operating budget from its endowment (Kelderman, 2009).

Heavy reliance on the institutional endowment can be a risky undertaking. With the onset of the economic downturn in the United States, a national survey reported an average of a 23 percent decline in institutional endowments in the last five months of the 2009 fiscal year (NACUBO, 2009). By the end of June 2009, it was estimated that Harvard's endowment had dropped 30 percent, causing university administrators to implement drastic budget cuts (Kelderman, 2009).

Thus, private colleges can find themselves in the precarious position of formulating an annual budget based on unreliable enrollment projections and endowment revenue in a volatile investment market. An overreliance on either enrollment or the endowment can spell financial disaster for any institution. Ideally, institutional leaders must seek a healthy balance between basing the institutional budget on student enrollment and endowment earnings.

Recruitment and Retention

Whether an institution is small or large, every SSAO ascribes to the notion that every student counts. Having worked at large institutions for most of my career, I know how hard my staff and I work to make sure that a student is more than just a number, but rather a complete individual who has personal needs, interests, and aspirations to which we must try to attend. Now that I am in a small school, my perspective has changed a bit. Every student really does count in a small institution—not only in a philosophical and environmental way, but in a very practical and financial way as well. Fluctuations in student enrollment at a small school have a much bigger impact on the institution; therefore, recruitment and retention of students is an ongoing part of everyone's job.

This is not to say that recruitment and retention were not a concern at the large institutions at which I worked. I participated in a variety of recruitment functions at my previous institutions and spent countless hours working with students to keep them in school and help them progress to graduation. Yet with more than twenty thousand admission applications for a freshman class of five thousand students, I often felt I spent more time assuaging students and their families regarding the limited number of students admitted and advising them of other educational opportunities available in the state. Certainly selectivity plays into this equation, but the sheer volume of students made it a much different situation.

At a small college, student enrollment is a constantly monitored data point. Application numbers and admissions deposits and withdrawals are reviewed and discussed by cabinet members almost weekly. Faculty and staff alike are routinely engaged in the campus visits, speaking to individual students and their families about the programs and resources available at the college. Similarly, it is not unusual to receive a call from a faculty member expressing concern about a student who has been missing class recently and being asked to assist in some individual follow-up with the student. Clearly the recruitment and retention of students is a conscious and intentional part of everyone's job at the college.

It is with this emphasis on recruitment and retention of students in mind that SSAOs must carefully assess their budgets during difficult economic times. If cuts are to be made, programs and services that directly support the recruitment and retention of students need to be protected because they are essential to the overall operations of the college. In particular, student affairs programs and services linked with student retention become the focus of departments throughout the division.

Small Changes Can Make Big Difference

In much the same way that the retention or loss of one student can make a difference, small changes that can generate cost savings or provide additional revenue can make a big difference at a small college. I was reminded of this when I recently began to review some user fees assessed by various departments within the division. In particular, vehicle registration fees and parking fines were relatively low compared to what I was familiar with at other institutions. These fees had not been changed within the last ten years, and some staff members requested we consider increasing in them. The rationale was not just about generating additional revenue, but more to serve as a deterrent to the growing number of parking violations on campus. In considering this change, I asked these staff members to use historical data to provide me with projections of the additional income these changes would generate, as well as the resulting change in the rate of violations. The data indicated that a marginal change in the violation rate could be achieved with a minimal increase in the user fees, but the amount of revenue generated for the entire fiscal year would be less than forty thousand dollars.

Recognizing the ill will that such fee increases would create within the campus community, particularly during challenging economic times, I began to question whether such a change was really worth it. Although a small improvement might be made in the campus parking situation, it was only forty thousand dollars, which was not much in relation to the overall college budget. In considering this change, I shared the information with another cabinet member. My colleague quickly reminded me that while forty thousand dollars might not be much at a large school, it represented one fewer student we had to guarantee to recruit in our enrollment projection. This insight shed a whole new light on my decision, and I submitted the recommendation to approve the parking fee increase.

With this new perspective, we began to look more closely at our expenses and soon identified ways to trim costs and generate small savings. Particularly at small colleges, small savings can make a big difference.

Conclusion

Although the importance of strategic planning and the use of various budgeting models are applicable across different types of institutions, there are some key differences between large universities and small colleges. Tuition calculations, discount rates, balancing enrollment versus the endowment, the importance of recruitment and retention, and the ability to make small changes to achieve big results are but a few of these differences. These issues, discussed briefly in this chapter, represent the personal reflections and observations of one professional who has recently made the transition from large public institutions to a small private college and should be viewed in this context. At the same time, I hope that they help to illustrate

NEW DIRECTIONS FOR STUDENT SERVICES • DOI: 10.1002/ss

some of the unique considerations and challenges SSAOs at small and private colleges face in the institutional budgeting process.

References

Hoover, E. "The State of College Admission: Full of Uncertainty." *Chronicle of Higher Education*, Oct. 20, 2009. Retrieved Oct. 20, 2009, from http://chronicle.com/article/The-State-of-College/48877/?sid=at&utm_source=at&utm_medium=en.

Kelderman, E. "Public and Private Colleges Feel Ripples of Wall Street's Woes." *Chronicle of Higher Education*, Aug. 24, 2009. Retrieved Oct. 28, 2009, from http://chronicle.com/article/Northeast-Colleges-Feel-Ri/48150/.

Krause, R. "Schools Do Have Better Buys." *Investor's Business Daily*, Sept. 25, 2009. Retrieved Oct. 22, 2009, from http://www.investors.com/NewsAndAnalysis/Article.aspx?id=507142.

NACUBO. *2008 NACUBO Endowment Study*. 2008. Retrieved Oct. 28, 2009, from http://www.nacubo.org/Research/NACUBO_Endowment_Study/Public_NES_Tables_.html.

Stripling, J. "Don't (Dis)count Them Out." *Inside Higher Ed*, Sept. 21, 2009. Retrieved Oct. 22, 2009, from http://www.insidehighered.com/news/2009/09/21/marymount.

Tharp, C. "Growing the Endowment in a High Risk Environment." In J. L. Yeager and others (eds.), *ASHE Reader on Finance in Higher Education*. (2nd ed.) Boston: Pearson Custom Publishing, 2001.

University of Florida. "Student Fee Calculation Estimate for Fall 2009 Students for the 2009–2010 Academic Year." Retrieved Oct. 22, 2009, from http://www.fa.ufl.edu/ufs/cashiers/fee-tier-ay2009–20098.asp.

EUGENE L. ZDZIARSKI II is vice president for student affairs and dean of students at Roanoke College in Salem, Virginia.

NEW DIRECTIONS FOR STUDENT SERVICES • DOI: 10.1002/ss

3

This chapter describes revenue-generating and cost-saving strategies that student affairs divisions may consider during periods of budget rescissions and categorizes them according to the decision-making entities involved in each. The chapter also explains why particular examples are well suited to individual institutions.

Alternate Budgetary Sources During Budget Rescissions

Kurt Keppler

It is hard to chuckle at the adage that public institutions are state located rather than state supported. Viewing the increase of tuition and fees as a solution for diminishing fiscal resources is no longer appropriate at most public institutions, nor are many other traditional methods of generating revenue and reducing costs. The perennial mantra of doing more with less has become completely unrealistic in many cases. On many campuses, divisions of student affairs should challenge rather than accept the budgetary hand that is dealt them, striving to creatively supplement their traditional sources of revenue. Simply accepting the allocated portion of the institution's state appropriations and general funds (usually derived from tuition and fees) is no longer enough. Throughout the past decade, many divisions have increased fundraising efforts and grant-writing initiatives and increased various fees for services. Still, it is now evident that student affairs must be even more aggressive and innovative in seeking alternative funding methods. The reason is clear: without supplemental funding, programs will be eliminated, services reduced, and layoffs imminent. This chapter reviews several strategies that might aid student affairs divisions in successfully managing budget reductions in ways that visibly reinforce the division's alignment with the overall mission and values of their institution.

Budget cuts are not new to student affairs practitioners; rarely a fiscal year passes without some type of cut or restructuring. Although the cutting process has gone by various names, pots of money are moved around, and theoretically some money is saved; however, the current and forthcoming

New Directions for Student Services, no. 129, Spring 2010   © Wiley Periodicals, Inc.
Published online in Wiley InterScience (www.interscience.wiley.com) • DOI: 10.1002/ss.349

cuts facing most institutions across America are hard, deep, and potentially permanent, and they will require rethinking and reorganizing on a level most student affairs professionals have not previously encountered.

Dealing with reduced sources of revenue means increased costs will be passed along not only to the users of university services—the students—but to many faculty and staff who will face furloughs and job loss, which will together create the type of unhappiness and unrest that typically gets passed along to student affairs divisions. Difficult and often unpopular decisions will have to be made, and some of the budgeting options outlined in this chapter will undoubtedly be exactly that. Effective, strategically minded senior student affairs officers (SSAOs) can, however, take some consolation that their decisions and influence are aligned with university missions and goals, and they are doing what is best for their institution in both the short and long terms.

The revenue-generating and cost-saving measures outlined in this chapter come from field experience, case studies from specific universities and colleges, and hypothetical situations based on real situations.

This chapter first focuses on funding sources and budget decisions over which student affairs divisions typically have little control (tuition and the various mandatory fees paid by all students), their political implications, and how they are affected during an economic recession. It then addresses cross-divisional budgeting decisions that can be made cooperatively by campus leadership, keeping in mind that not every alternative is an option for every school. Next, the chapter covers revenue-generating and cost-saving measures that may be implemented by a student affairs division essentially on its own. The chapter concludes with some discussion on the costs versus benefits of the various cutback strategies and the need for creative thinking during difficult fiscal periods. A series of recommendations are offered to help budget managers cope with the results of budgetary reductions, so that they may be able to manage the institutional rumor mill, focus on clear communication with key constituent groups, and maintain crucial student services.

Budget Decisions Typically Involving Governing Bodies

Before moving to methods on which student affairs is likely to have more influence, I review some budget factors over which student affairs often has little or no influence. The methods identified in this section require significant review and are driven by legislative or governing board decisions. In the best case, where SSAOs are particularly influential with the university president or the provost for academic affairs, he or she may be able to affect these decisions to some degree by recommendations; none of these budgeting choices, however, is made by a leader acting in isolation.

Raising Tuition. Ultimately tuition increase decisions are shaped by many factors: institutional mission, board policy, recent increases, comparative costs at peer institutions, and scholarship opportunities. In terms of financial support or trickle-down, increased tuition may have little impact on student affairs divisions that are predominantly financed from non-general funds. Conversely, it may have more impact on divisions whose budget comes primarily from general funds. Although increases in tuition may be politically difficult for student affairs, since objecting parents and students often use student affairs offices to voice their concerns, increased tuition costs are becoming a universal reality in educational systems across the nation. And in many cases, the increased revenue from tuition is still nowhere near enough to fully support current offerings and services.

Enrollment. An SSAO can sometimes moderately or significantly influence enrollment decisions. As with tuition and user fees, however, this decision is likely to require the approval of the board of trustees, president, or provost, or some combination of these.

Enrollment Growth. It seems logical and obvious that increased enrollment would provide additional tuition and fee revenue, and henceforth help lower the impact of impending cuts. However, whether this is the case is institution specific.

Private schools often benefit from increasing enrollment because they get to retain and use the fees and tuition that students pay. Increased enrollment also benefits public institutions where the state is giving a subsidy or appropriation for the realized increase. It is also worth mentioning that increasing enrollment should be an option only if the capacity to do so already exists; there should be both physical and human infrastructure in place and available for "extra" students to use and access.

Enrollment Shrinkage. When institutional capacity does not exist or the actual revenue accrued by the added bodies does not counter the cost of serving additional students, such as public schools without state appropriations for enrollment growth, enrollment shrinkage may occur. Enrollment shrinkage will occur at private schools with no capacity to grow and at public schools where state appropriations for increased enrollment do not exist. In such cases, campuses may force an enrollment reduction by implementing more rigorous admission standards or by system mandates. Theoretically such action decreases the pool of eligible students, thereby mitigating the demand on fiscal and human resources.

Class Size Ratios. Class size ratios generally grow out of enrollment decisions. A larger faculty-to-student ratio results when enrollment increases and faculty hiring stay constant; in this case, an institution may add certain large or "supersection" courses when it is pedagogically viable. These measures are effective only if the large classes fill. There may be political ramifications to such an approach as well, but divisions of student affairs will likely have little influence over class-size-ratio decisions.

Increasing Fees. The system for fee collection and implementation varies from campus to campus and fee to fee. Some fees commonly referred to as comprehensive or mandatory are paid, along with tuition, by every student for services that they may either use or not use at their own prerogative. Examples are student activities fees, health center fees, athletic fees, and technology fees.

On most colleges, all students pay the same activities fee regardless of how many clubs they join or how many events they attend. The same occurs with most technology fees. Typically all students pay the same technology fee whether they are online eighteen hours a day or two hours a week.

Adjusting systemwide or campuswide fees such as these usually requires approval by the president and sometimes the board of trustees. (A plethora of other user fees that might be more campus or division directed are discussed in a later section.) Increasing user fees for particular services, and implementing mandatory one-time, temporary, or permanent fees required of all students can play a significant role in budget reduction strategies; however, political ramifications may be associated with such increases.

Existing User Fees. Existing user fees may be increased to cover budget shortfalls. Sometimes their revenue is used not only in the division in which they are collected, but in other interrelated cost centers as well, an action that often requires cross-divisional planning and cooperation, and perhaps even require sanctioning by the state legislature or the board of trustees.

One-Time or Temporary Mandatory Fees. Sometimes a special fee with a limited lifetime can be implemented as an emergency measure. In contrast to new permanent mandatory fees, this fee may be more flexible to use and easier for the board of trustees or legislature to approve. For example, the University of Georgia System implemented a temporary fee of one hundred dollars in fall 2008 that all students were required to pay. It was not an earmarked fee, did not have a mandatory use, and was not permanent; in addition, there was no timeline for its removal. Such fees are helpful to reduce across-the-board cuts and delay or reduce the need for layoffs. Despite their flexibility, these types of fees are controversial. Students do not plan for them, so they are unanticipated and susceptible to much criticism. Although they may not be sustainable, they may be necessary short-term solutions, especially when raising tuition is politically inappropriate, financially imprudent, or otherwise impossible.

Increased Use of Technology. Many institutions have long abandoned the printed school, hard-copy class registration booklet, and bound student handbook. On many campuses, these have been replaced by compact discs, e-files linked to a variety of departmental Web sites, or both. A perusal of institutional Web sites confirms that virtual tours, student-developed videos, and online newsletters have replaced many traditional viewbooks and departmental brochures. Although individual departments can implement the use of technology on their own once the overall infrastructure is in place, the initial funding for such infrastructure nearly always requires approval by the board of trustees and other governing entities.

Using technology to complement or supplant traditional methods can lower operating costs and bring about other pedagogical and mission-based benefits as well. For example, a tactic that may not only save money but also boost retention is using a Web-based student communication tool.

NEW DIRECTIONS FOR STUDENT SERVICES • DOI: 10.1002/ss

One such program developed by EducationDynamics (Troy and Thomassi, 2009) works as an internal social networking device that provides a variety of educational interaction, such as personal and academic counseling, self-assessment, and advising, to students with a user-specific secure Web site. EducationDynamics uses this description of its freshman retention module, FYRe: "This program provides the optimal communications vehicle to encourage involvement in campus and residential life. It lets students explore support services and resources on their own time and in their preferred medium: the Web. The program's lively content helps students troubleshoot a wide range of personal and academic issues, while directing them to campus and Web resources that address everything from homesickness to test anxiety to resolving roommate and relationship woes" (EducationDynamics Heuristics, cited by Troy and Tomassi, 2009). Self-assessment modules allow students to gauge potential problems, while the Student Service Center offers a confidential platform through which they can ask questions or voice concerns. In this example, a technological mechanism provided students with services that otherwise may have been delivered by advisors or counselors in face-to-face meetings and appointments. The traditional personal modes of delivery may be less cost efficient and harder to sustain in difficult economies. And in fact, most students today are quite comfortable using and accessing e-communication and Web-based programs, which creates an excellent trade-off.

Summing Up. There is no guarantee that any real savings have accrued directly to student affairs from the changes outlined. Therefore, these strategies may be best conceived as a potential means of mitigating institutional shortfalls rather than divisional ones. The next grouping of strategies may provide relief directly to student affairs divisions, and they represent areas over which student affairs has more significant influence.

Measures That Can Be Implemented with Campus-Based Decisions

On most campuses, the strategies explored here do not require approval by the board of trustees or state legislatures. Typically these approaches are initiated by SSAOs working in concert with other university leaders. Although these strategies might be easier to implement in one respect, they still require significant planning and cooperation between divisions, such as student affairs and academic affairs, and student affairs and business and administration, development and advancement, and human resources. It is especially important in trying budget times that SSAOs not only be aware of where revenue comes from and which divisions make certain budgeting decisions, but also to take campus partnerships more seriously than ever before.

Increasing User Fees. On most campuses a number of services are funded completely by user fees paid by the consumer of the service or program. In these cases, the user receives a direct, tangible service—such as obtaining official copies of transcripts, securing the right to park in designated ramps or lots, and entering the dining hall or eateries to enjoy any number of prepaid meals. User fees differ from comprehensive fees such as student activity or athletic fees that are typically mandatory and approved by the board of trustees regardless of an individual's real or perceived use of the service. Generally user fees can be adjusted by the division that offers the service, sometimes in consultation with a student fee advisory committee.

Permanent User Fees. Adding new permanent and ongoing user fees is a possibility during university budget shortfalls. Until recently many institutions have offered certain services on campus free of cost. In difficult financial times, it may become necessary or prudent to charge users for these services. Such a decision can be very unpopular, since the service has had a tradition of being free. In spite of users' reactions, implementing a new fee may nevertheless be a reasonable means of accumulating anticipated revenue. Examples of such a strategy include charging for printing in computer labs and fees for replacement campus ID cards. The campus entities with a stake in the services and fees must decide if the revenue gained is worth the negative reactions induced by the dollars raised.

Transferring Budgetary Responsibilities to Fee-Based Departments. Sometimes student affairs divisions have opportunities to use funding mechanisms derived from sources outside the typical general budget. For example, when I was the dean of students at a large metropolitan institution, a critical budget deficit was partially addressed by shifting salary costs to fee-based or auxiliary budgets. A justifiable place to save student affairs' general funds during this particular deficit was in the case of a director of student activities. This director had been paid by state-appropriated dollars and spent the majority of her time working with student organizations and student events. I shifted an appropriate percentage of her salary and benefit package to a student union budget that was funded primarily by mandatory student fees. A budget move such as this allows the cost of that staff person's salary and benefits to be absorbed by a self-support unit that arguably should help support the part of the position that assists or supervises the unit.

This strategy has some disadvantages: the self-support budget may already be lean, or the leaders involved in allocating fees may be philosophically opposed to the concept. In difficult economic times, positions, duties, salaries, or benefits may have already been absorbed by other departments. Nevertheless, these types of shifts should be considered where available.

Revenues Accrued by Auxiliaries. Frequently student affairs divisions depend on monies attained from a variety of auxiliary revenues. Some auxiliaries generate a great deal of money, such as room rental fees in departments of housing, revenues generated by university unions, and revenues generated by student government organizations, which may even be their own nonprofit corporation (as in the California State University system). Some smaller sources of auxiliary revenue may come from testing center fees, for example, or parents' association fees. There is no uniform campus-to-campus expectation of how such fees are generated, augmented, and used; therefore, SSAOs should be knowledgeable about their particular campus and be proactive in forging cost-saving and revenue-generating opportunities related to such fees.

These auxiliary revenues can be helpful in mitigating budget reductions, since many administrators use these types of funds to sustain programs and services that are in financial jeopardy. Similar to the funds generated by fee-based departments, auxiliary-generated revenues may be shared with other campus units in lean times. There are few limits to the possibilities of cross-divisional revenue sharing; campus leaders are mainly limited by their knowledge and ability to seek out mutually advantageous options.

Merging of Departments. Although the merging of departments or services is common within divisions of student affairs, mergers between divisions are also a possibility that should not be overlooked. Sometimes a merger of two or more small offices can create an economy of scale that saves money without much reduction in service provision. Combining two small offices—for example, alcohol education and health promotions—may allow for a shared receptionist, a joint marketing campaign, and collaborative use of peer educators. As an added and unintended positive point, it may even increase the visibility of the services on campus. As is always the case, there are some counter-issues to consider, in particular, space needs and mission alignment.

Delayed Facility Improvements or Renovations. Most campuses have governing board–approved master plans for facility expansion and infrastructure improvements. Reduced budgets may delay scheduled facility renovations or reduce expansion plans. These kinds of delays or deferred maintenance are a cross-divisional decision on many campuses. Consider the maintenance and renovation of a building that physically houses the offices affiliated with student affairs. Any decision to defer maintenance or renovation to the student services building is likely to involve physical plant, maintenance, and the vice presidents for business affairs and student affairs. When these kinds of reductions or cutbacks are being considered, each move should be made in a purposeful, mission-driven way, despite the fact that deferring maintenance or postponing renovations may appear on the surface to be easy and straightforward decisions.

Postponing New Programs Indefinitely. As with facility improvements or renovations, a recessionary economic environment is not the best time for program expansion; however, the university's mission statement and strategic plan should still guide the choice to indefinitely postpone a proposed new program. Less relevant spending, for example, could be cut to keep intact a burgeoning program that better supports the university's mission. Unless an institution has restricted funds that are designated specifically for a new program, the chances of moving ahead with new programs or services are minimal when cutbacks are in order. This does not mean that

NEW DIRECTIONS FOR STUDENT SERVICES • DOI: 10.1002/ss

proposed programs should be eliminated without scrutiny and deliberate choices. Early in trying economic times, there may still be some budget fat that could be trimmed before an efficient new program is put on hold.

Revenue Sources and Cost-Saving Measures Within Student Affairs

The following revenue-generating and cost-saving measures can usually be implemented by one or more departments within the division of student affairs. Here, the division or the departments can design and implement procedures by consulting with the SSAO and relevant staff members.

Increased Use of Paraprofessionals. Part-time paraprofessionals can significantly supplement staffing needs in divisions of student affairs. Many campuses have used this option already and may not have additional areas where further implementation is appropriate. However, universities have tremendous human resources that can often be expanded, in particular, graduate students, retirees, volunteers, and interns. In each of these paraprofessional situations described next, there may be cost savings to the department. But the savings may come at some cost since supervision is always required.

Graduate Assistants. On my campus, graduate assistants (GAs) are considered to be .33 full-time equivalents and assigned to departments to work on the average 13.3 hours weekly. The Division of Student Affairs uses approximately thirty GAs each year, and by pure work hours, this accounts for ten full-time positions. The office receives a motivated, energetic paraprofessional at significantly less cost than one-third of a full-time professional's salary. Departments do not have responsibility for GA benefits, and the student receives a stipend and tuition waiver (particularly beneficial for nonresidents).

Graduate assistants may not be appropriate in all units. They may not have the experience to do all duties assigned to entry-level professional staff, and they also require supervisory time and evaluation, which places some demands on the assigned supervisor who is already likely doing more with less. Still, at least in financial terms, GAs are often a win-win solution.

Retirees. Retirement in today's financial environment is a risky decision at best. Many staff have postponed retirement after losing money associated with their retirement investments. Two issues are at stake when contemplating hiring a recent retiree: one budgetary and one career related. It is obvious that employees who have worked at the institution for thirty or more years draw larger salaries than new employees, so it may be in the institution's best financial interest to increase the number of retirees during a fiscal crisis. Even after retirement incentives, the campus can rehire a less expensive replacement, keep the post vacant, or eliminate the position. In many instances, however, retirees desire to remain with the institution in some capacity. Retirement may be attractive to them for a number of reasons, but they may also wish to have some part-time employment. To address this, the University of Georgia System offers a

NEW DIRECTIONS FOR STUDENT SERVICES • DOI: 10.1002/ss

partial retirement program. There, an employee may officially retire at full benefits. After a short hiatus, she can be rehired at 49 percent of her previous salary and work half-time at the institution. This is not an entitlement program, and the employee's supervisor must approve the rehiring. Yet in many situations, this is another win-win opportunity: the campus retains an experienced employee at half salary, and the rehired employee feels valued and appreciated.

Internships. Other low-cost staffing options for student affairs departments to consider are interns and co-op students. In most internships, there is both a supervisory or experiential component and an academic component. Paid internships exist on some campuses. On others, the intern works for academic credit as part of a curricular requirement. In this case, the student is simultaneously providing a service to the supervising office and benefiting from the educational experience. Offices that expand their use of interns may be able to postpone the reduction of full-time staff positions. Interns generally cannot take the place of a professional because they likely do not have the experience, licensure, or training. Nonetheless, interns may reduce salary costs associated with more qualified full-time employees. In addition, they may provide extended hours of operation in facilities like recreation centers and student unions. An office such as the counseling center often depends heavily on graduate interns who need specific professional supervision before they meet their curricular requirements. In each of the paraprofessional situations described above, there may be cost savings to the department. But the "savings" may come at some "cost" since supervision is always required.

Staff Contracts and Job Definitions. In addition to using paraprofessionals, other personnel cost-saving opportunities may be found in three areas: job rotation, temporary job restructuring, and ten-month contracts.

Job Rotation. Many student affairs units or departments have predictably busy periods throughout the year. The intense pressure and activity times may ebb and flow with less hectic and lower demand times. A possible savings may occur if departments rotate staff during demanding periods and rotate them out in slower periods. A staff member may be hired exactly for that purpose. Perhaps an employee is hired to rotate between financial aid and career services. This employee may work in financial aid during the hectic April through August months as a loan specialist. During other periods, she may serve as a counselor with career services. Using this concept to a lesser degree, an administrator may ask a staff member who primarily is responsible for a specific area, say, Greek affairs, to work summer orientation during key weeks in the summer. In either case, using staff more efficiently may save some dollars.

Temporary Job Restructuring. Occasionally an administrator will need to alter or adjust the responsibilities of a staff member both to fulfill critical unit needs and reduce costs. In these circumstances, it may be possible to use a swing person who is hired for a critical need in advising to be temporarily reassigned to the registrar's office. Or an area coordinator could be hired within residential life who has strong writing skills and a background in alcohol education. If there is an increase in alcohol–related vandalism, the director could be asked to spend time in June and July working with a faculty member on a federal grant designed for peer training in vandalism reduction. Here, a portion of the area coordinator's salary could be absorbed by the grant. The division ultimately saves some salary funds during a less hectic period for residence life.

Ten-Month Appointment. In this situation, the department head offers to reduce some positions to ten months. This allows the employee to work five-sixths of the work year at 83 percent of her salary. This may be attractive to some employees, for example, those who would like to have their summers off so that they can be home during the summer break with their young children. This may be another win-win solution, since it will yield some salary savings. Obviously this works only with certain positions, and the human resource office on campus may have some contractual provisions that must be approved in advance.

Parents' Associations and Councils. During the past decade, parents have become increasingly involved in their child's college experience. Many institutions are harnessing this parental interest by creating positive ways for active parents to be involved in associations and councils (Keppler, Mullendore, and Carey, 2005; Farber, 2009). This can be another win-win situation for student affairs. The division can generate revenue from the parent councils, and interested parents can provide insights and observations regarding the undergraduate experience. Parents' associations are similar to the K–12 Parent Teachers Association (PTA). Parents become members of the association by paying dues and generally receive low-cost benefits: newsletters, bookstore or athletic ticket discounts, windshield stickers, and so on. At Valdosta State, for example, the Parents' Council, a subset of the Parent's Association, entitled established by-laws and guidelines for use of association dues. The Parents' Council approved the use of association funds for student emergencies and student leadership development, among other things. As membership increases, the revenues from dues grow as well. This allows the institution to tap nongeneral funds for things like expanding the leadership development program. Parents' Council members or association officers can be good fundraisers as well, and many campuses have been effective in raising monies through parent groups.

Fundraising. Fundraising activities solicit donations from external donors that can supplement operating budgets. Emergent fundraising programs often require fundraising staff to bring in at least the same amount of dollars that match their salary. In more established programs, fundraisers may be expected to land gifts that exceed their salary by a certain percentage. The Education Advisory Board, in a publication for the Student Affairs Leadership Council, provides extensive detail on student affairs fundraising and shares examples of successful programs. The publication offers sound advice on designing and implementing a student affairs fundraising program and outlines a variety of different structures and approaches for strategizing your "asking philosophy" (Education Advisory Board, 2009).

Grant Writing. Many academic professionals might think that grant opportunities are diminished in poor economic times, but data do not substantiate that perception. A variety of grant opportunities are available that may be appropriate for student affairs divisions. Among the sources of grants are state and federal government, private foundations, corporations and businesses, and nonprofit agencies, each with specific guidelines and restrictions pertaining to both the application process and the implementation of an awarded grant. The Web site www.grants.gov is a free resource that can help grant seekers identify federal financial assistance. In addition, many universities have subscriptions to proprietary databases that delineate federal opportunities and programs operated by foundations and nonprofit organizations. Among these are InfoEd's SPIN (Sponsored Programs Information System), IRIS (Illinois Researcher Information System), and COS (Community of Science). These systems allow the individual to set up a user profile, and he or she is notified by e-mail each time a funding opportunity that matches his or her interests is added or updated.

Student affairs divisions should develop relationships with their campus's sponsored programs office for help identifying funding sources as well as for assistance in proposal preparation and submission. Sponsored programs can also help coordinate with the university's foundation in seeking funding from a private foundation or corporation.

Partnering with Other Institutions. Another cost-saving strategy for student affairs professionals to consider is establishing partnerships with proximate universities. At first glance, such collaborations may seem unrealistic, but some institutions are located in towns or cities with closely clustered colleges or universities. Student affairs administrators from adjacent institutions could identify opportunities where students from both campuses might jointly participate in a program or share a facility.

Community Collaborative Efforts. Other colleges and universities are located in small and midsized rural communities where the institution has resources that are minimally available elsewhere. Student affairs sponsors functions that lend themselves to community collaboration, such as day camps, diversity programs, film series, leadership training, swim lessons, and career counseling. Although similar partnerships may already be in place through the office of continuing education, there may be additional opportunities to generate some revenue by opening select student affairs programs and services to community participants.

Outsourcing to the Private Sector. More possible financial savings may result by contracting out specific services, or outsourcing them, to specialized agencies external to the university. This is not a new concept. The outsourcing of food services to companies like Marriott and Sodexo and bookstores to companies like Follet and Barnes & Noble is commonplace on most campuses. Similar arrangements are not unusual for a wide variety of other functions, including health services, outcomes assessment, and housing. Student affairs professionals should engage in adequate research and full due diligence before they outsource internal programs. They should inquire about the possibility of transferring competent staff to the external company's payroll. And they should understand thoroughly contractual agreements related to employee workload, product quality, and consumer costs. In many cases, the quality and breadth of service increase after a program has been outsourced. An example of a mutually beneficial arrangement with the private sector could be the Women's Center partnering with a local YWCA to offer twenty-four-hour rape crisis counseling; the two entities could share staff, funding, and perhaps a common space or office.

Recommendations and Conclusions

Serious budgetary cutbacks always bring challenges. During these periods, administrators carefully review every program, service, and dollar spent. Accountability may be harder to address in student affairs work, since it is difficult to determine the exact resources necessary to achieve the desired student outcome.

One of the best ways to get through a budget crisis is for all interested stakeholders to be grounded in and committed to the same strategic plan, mission, and values. This chapter builds on Chapter One, which describes what SSAOs need to understand and do in terms of division and campuswide budgeting. By understanding the budgeting process and the options for generating, combining, and allocating resources, student affairs managers can better demonstrate the rationale used, and data examined, so stakeholders will be clearer on why specific decisions were made. Decision making at this level does not occur in a vacuum, and informed, purposeful leaders can negotiate, advocate, and affect many cost-saving and revenue-generating measures across divisions and entire campuses.

The budget reduction plan must be communicated appropriately to the campus or division (see Chapter Four). Clearly every institution has a different approach to disseminating sensitive information to its constituents. Process can be as important as, and possibly more so than, the actual decision. Staff want to be informed about the rationale used to design reduction scenarios. Whether the approach is a letter from the vice president (or president), a series of visits with departments, a town hall meeting, or other method of presentation, sharing the procedures used in determining cutbacks is advantageous.

Every campus faces unique fiscal and political challenges; the institutional mission may suggest which approaches are best suited to a particular situation. A large comprehensive public institution may have more flexibility with enrollment strategies than a small liberal arts institution that depends exclusively on a hard-to-negotiate target enrollment number. Institutions with a large part-time and nontraditional enrollment may choose

NEW DIRECTIONS FOR STUDENT SERVICES • DOI: 10.1002/ss

different strategies from campuses with a high percentage of resident students who demand comprehensive student activities programs. University leaders must know their own institutions intimately and the options available to them. This chapter has addressed every question about possible budgeting options and provides a framework for the questions that managers might begin to ask to know more.

References

Education Advisory Board. *Managing Through the Downturn: Strategies for Cost-Cutting and Revenue Generation in Student Affairs Organizations.* Washington, D.C.: Advisory Board Company, 2009.

Farber, A. *College: What Parents Need to Know.* Dayton, Ohio: Woodburn Press, 2009.

Keppler, K. J., Mullendore, R. M., and Carey, A. *Partnering with Parents of Today's College Students.* Washington, D.C.: NASPA, 2005.

Troy, A., and Tomassi, P. "EducationDynamics." July 30, 2009, Retrieved Sept. 2, 2009, from http://www.educationdynamics.com/Company/about-us/.

KURT KEPPLER is vice president for student affairs at Valdosta State University in Georgia.

NEW DIRECTIONS FOR STUDENT SERVICES • DOI: 10.1002/ss

4

Understanding the institutional context of financial issues and related communication enhances the effectiveness of student affairs administrators within their areas of responsibility and as leaders of change on campus. This chapter focuses on key aspects of developing a comprehensive communication strategy.

Communicating with Stakeholders

Jonathan Eldridge, Tisa Mason

Communicating with stakeholders is important in any crisis or time of change. Institutions with ongoing budget issues often deal with frustration, concern, and even panic on the part of various constituents, which can lead to enrollment degradation, funding reduction, and public questioning of priorities. A lack of communication can make matters worse. Ineffective communication might be most harmful of all because it can lead to rumors, misinformation, and second-guessing, and it can force the expenditure of time and energy on putting out fires rather than on tackling the real issues at hand.

A strong communication plan keeps stakeholders focused on strategic messages and minimizes the risk of collateral damage from tough decisions that need to be made to get the institution through fiscal challenges. It is imperative that an institution craft a comprehensive plan to address fiscal issues effectively. However, constituents who do not or cannot understand the plan, how it was developed, its implications, and why certain choices were made over others can compromise the plan's effectiveness.

Reducing or eliminating programs and positions is incredibly difficult work. Choosing between things that all have value and contribute in some way to the student experience will undoubtedly leave some stakeholders unhappy. With reductions in services come frustration. Students may ask why their fees have not gone down if they are getting less. Staff may complain that they are taking the brunt of frustration or taking on more work, perhaps even coupled with salary reductions or furlough days. Staff and faculty may feel a sense of loss as colleagues they have known and worked with for years are suddenly gone.

A strong communication plan can honor these feelings while managing the negative impact that tough decisions necessitate. Colleges and universities are largely known for commitments to shared governance and consensus building. Although this works well in guiding institutions forward over the long term, in times of crisis, it is often difficult to reach consensus, as someone is usually perceived as losing out. In financially challenging times, our instinct is often to look out for ourselves. At a university, this can manifest itself in departments' and programs' rallying support, making it politically unpleasant to cut them, or pointing out the faults of other areas. If decisions and process are not communicated effectively, the likelihood that one or more of these issues will manifest greatly increases.

Every campus is unique, with different histories, cultures, and circumstances. Nevertheless, certain items need to be considered when developing a communication strategy, regardless of institution. For example, what is the internal expectation of transparency in the budget process? The external expectation (public, press, and so on)? What has been the history with budget cuts in the past? Is there lingering resentment that might bleed into current discussions or decisions? Do people trust the accuracy of what is communicated? How involved in decisions do different constituents expect to be? Is there a good relationship with the local press? The student press? Student government? How involved are parents in the life of the campus? How involved are governing boards? The answers to these and other questions are unique for every institution, but every institution facing financial challenges must consider them carefully in order to minimize negative messaging and effectively communicate "how we got here," "what we are doing," and "where we are headed."

This chapter focuses on the following key areas and their roles in the development of a comprehensive communication strategy:

- Understanding and using institutional mission and planning
- Understanding campus culture and circumstance
- Understanding and using available resources
- Understanding and using available communication tools
- Addressing the different needs of various stakeholders
- Anticipating reactions and perpetuating the message

Understanding and Using Institutional Mission and Planning

Some institutions are better positioned than others to communicate difficult financial news and tough decisions because they are able to closely align cuts with institutional mission, the strategic plan, and previously stated priorities. Strategic planning, in addition to charting a collective trajectory for an institution, provides a framework from which to communicate decisions and their rationale. It is easier to get buy-in if people can see how the long-term plan and current reality connect. In the absence of a comprehensive strategic plan that delineates programmatic priorities, the institutional mission becomes increasingly critical. Do cuts align with the stated mission? If so, helping stakeholders come to terms with tough times becomes easier.

How effectively the institutional mission and planning can be used to communicate decisions depends on a number of factors. How well known, understood, and accepted is the institution's mission? How well connected to it are external stakeholders? If connection to the mission is lacking, perhaps a budget crisis can actually afford an opportunity to introduce—or reintroduce—core values and strategic directions.

At Fort Hays State University in Kansas, President Edward Hammond asked all budget cuts to align with five planning principles: serve students, keep costs down for students, protect faculty and staff, ask people to do more, and minimize the economic impact on Ellis County. The planning principles were emphasized consistently as decisions were being made and, more important, as they were being communicated.

What if cuts don't align with stated priorities? As unfortunate as it may be, circumstances may result in the president or other leaders making decisions that do not readily align with the mission and goals. Opportunistic cuts, such as not filling a vacant position or sweeping excess funds in a key program, might actually contradict stated priorities or values. If this is the case, communicating cuts can be even more difficult. Honesty in acknowledging that principles are being compromised might also be difficult while remaining in unison with institutional leadership. However, if incongruence is obvious, not acknowledging it only invites speculation and mistrust.

Understanding and using institutional perspective through mission and planning become essential for successful navigation through a financial crisis. Those who use the crisis to first reinforce what the institution has already decided is important, and then to strengthen and reiterate its commitments to institutional vision, mission, and priorities, are bound to find more resilience and support than those who do not.

Understanding Campus Culture and Circumstance

By providing adequate context, we can often temper reactions to negative news and difficult times. People may understand what decisions have been made, but without understanding why they were made, they may have difficulty supporting them. In order to effectively communicate the reasoning behind strategies in response to fiscal realities, we must provide clear answers to certain questions relating to campus culture and circumstance.

What is the campus culture? Should messages about budget cuts be crafted so as to honor traditions? Anticipate reactions? Mold support? The answers to these questions might depend on the kinds of changes that are needed. Is the change really necessary (budget reductions), or is it a matter of choice (new leadership or new directions, for example)? What are the consequences of not making change? How imminent are those consequences? How well can they be quantified and articulated? These questions may seem daunting, but every institution has an answer to each of them, and those answers must be understood in advance of determining how to frame communication.

At Southern Oregon University (SOU), years of continuing reductions in state funding have left faculty and staff feeling demoralized and undervalued. Although they remain committed to student and institutional success, it has become difficult for senior administrators to convince anyone that better times are ahead and that additional cuts, undertaken strategically, will pay off. A ten-year culture of reduction sets a very different starting point for discussion from one that emerges from an institution that has enjoyed financial stability over the past decade. It is feasible to think it might be harder to communicate additional cuts at SOU than elsewhere. As unfortunate as it may be, budget cuts as an ongoing part of SOU's culture actually create the familiarity with causes and effects that might not exist elsewhere. At an institution accustomed to ample resources, cuts of any size or kind may be met with shock and disbelief, making an understanding of the situation harder to communicate.

This begs the question, "How much change can we tolerate?" An institution may not have control over how much change or how many budget cuts it needs to make. But understanding whether cuts fall within or exceed the perceived change threshold is another key element of campus culture to consider.

The following factors are also important to an institution's change threshold:

- How has change been received in the past?
- Have past changes resulted in improvements, or have they been seen as ineffectual?
- Has change been occurring often—and maybe too often?
- Has it needed to occur but has not?

The answers to these questions can determine the tenor of communications. If a community sees responses to past financial or other major issues as ineffective, it may be wise to spend extra effort detailing how current plans are different, how data are now being used more effectively, or how the institution is now obtaining more information from key constituents. In addition, acknowledging past efforts on the part of staff, faculty, and others—and that additional reductions really are not fair given the past hard work—can go a long way to expand the change threshold of a campus. If we show an understanding of people's realities, we can temper the "here-we-go-again" syndrome that often leads to more negativity.

NEW DIRECTIONS FOR STUDENT SERVICES • DOI: 10.1002/ss

Taking the time to understand and appreciate the factors that make up the climate and culture of a campus regarding budget issues and financial difficulties will help ensure that the development of a communications strategy is congruent with campus reality—and thus anticipate reactions from all constituents. Along with a clear understanding and articulation of core values, institution-specific answers to questions of culture begin to make the foundation of a solid communication strategy.

Understanding and Using Available Resources

Every campus enters a financial crisis with certain resources. Faculty and staff are perhaps the most valuable resources (and, unfortunately, one of the most expensive). Physical and financial assets are also resources. Certainly students are a key resource, even if looked at solely from an enrollment-equals-revenue standpoint. Beyond the very pragmatic view of these and other resources, institutions have less tangible resources that play critical roles in weathering financial storms and formulating effective communications strategies. This section focuses on three of these less tangible resources that play major roles in effective communication:

- Informal campus leadership
- Institutional data
- Institutional processes

Informal Campus Leadership. It is important to understand beyond the organizational chart what leadership is in place to carry out change. Certainly the president, vice presidents, deans, department chairs, faculty leaders and others will be expected to help the campus community make sense of what is taking place. Yet every campus community also has members who carry more influence than others, regardless of their positions. Who is always in the know about campus events (and campus gossip)? Which staff has their fingers on the pulse of the campus rumor mill? Are there faculty who may not be in formal leadership positions but who get everyone's attention and respect when they speak? Individuals who know the pulse of the campus, have the respect of their peers, can shape the campus discussion without committee membership or job title, or embody institutional memory are the informal leaders of a campus community.

These community members are a valuable resource. Suppose, for example, that for whatever reason, faculty and staff do not believe executive officers are telling them the truth or sharing the whole story, regardless of how many memos, how many Web pages, or how many campus meetings have been used to convey what is going on and why. Explaining the situation, financial or otherwise, to those people who have a way of getting the word out—and then allowing them to do just that—does not change the message, but it does change the messenger. And if the issue is one of trust, identifying who is trusted to be the messenger is very important. Of course, there has to be trust that the message will not be diluted or warped as it is conveyed through these informal channels.

Effectively engaging these informal leaders will both avoid their being off-message and create additional means of communicating to constituents. In order to use these individuals, it is important to know how well these informal leaders understand the issues at hand and their context. If the understanding is limited, then it is worthwhile to spend whatever time is necessary to expand it, as informal leaders may well convey information regardless of whether they are specifically asked to carry the message.

It is also important to know whether there is consensus among the institutional leadership and informal campus leaders on what needs to occur. In fact, there may very well be a lack of consensus amongst various informal leaders. If general consensus does not exist, it can be useful to bring informal leaders together to discuss their thoughts on the situation. Focus groups often provide valuable information and even the occasional "aha!" moment. They also provide an opportunity to convey accurate information that will likely find its way to a wider audience. Because someone is consulting with them makes them more likely to feel valued and part of the process, which will also pay dividends.

Institutional Data. Effective and accurate communication plans are based on reliable data that guide decision making and reinforce institutional priorities. Institutional data are wonderful resources on which to draw during a financial crisis. They can help paint a picture to legislators about how underfunded colleges are and about how an institution is doing amazingly well with what little it has. They can also paint a picture internally about progress that has been made—and thus should not be compromised as cuts unfold. And they can help debunk myths that might be standing in the way of getting buy-in on tough decisions.

Using institutional data effectively in communication efforts requires answering some questions:

- What data do you have?
- What do the data say about the severity of your situation?
- What do they say about productivity and accountability?
- Do the data reinforce or contradict any proposed actions?
- How do the data relate to core values and strategic plans?
- Are the data understandable to constituents affected by decisions?

The answers to these questions should be formulated and analyzed before decisions are made, and data should then be used in communicating the decisions that emerge.

Often in a financial crisis, stakeholders seek data that shore up their perspective, especially if programmatic or personnel cuts are likely to hit their area. In addition, they may challenge data that tell them something other than what they want to hear. Institutions with a strong, consistent history of data collection, analysis, and dissemination are well positioned to have data be an integral part of crisis communications. They are also more likely to have stakeholders who can interpret data accurately and consistently. Institutions that are not data driven may face challenges when using data to back up decisions. For example, there may be a lack of deeper understanding of the data and their contexts on the part of constituents and a resultant reluctance to believe the data, especially if they are used to support unpopular decisions.

Ultimately institutional data are a valuable resource if they are used to make sense of rapid or massive changes. A strong communication strategy will rely on institutional data to help tell the story of "how we got here," "what we are doing," and "where we are headed." In other words, data can illustrate that "we got here" because of, for example, declining enrollments, which came about because of reduced scholarship capacity, which resulted from significant endowment losses. Data can also support "what we are doing"—targeting lower-need students within the institution's geographical reach and offering them small scholarships they traditionally would not have received in the past in order to increase yield and thus bolster enrollment. Finally, data can be used to help track and assess efforts undertaken—the "where we are going" of the equation. To carry the enrollment example to its conclusion, new enrollment targets have been established and success will be measured by reaching them within the newly limited financial aid budget, while monitoring traditional indicators of institutional health such as academic quality in the applicant pool.

Established Institutional Processes. Established institutional processes may be considered as resources when formulating a crisis communication plan. Institutions with well-established and accepted means of involving constituents in decision making have an advantage in difficult times. In fact, these processes can act as a script for how best to communicate.

Does the institution have an established, methodical annual budget process that involves people from across units and divisions? If so, and if this method is not abandoned in a time of crisis, then it can be relied on not only to help determine a course of action but to communicate it as well. This is especially true if the annual budget process already has communication strategies built in, such as posting minutes of meetings to the Web, conducting open meetings, or providing regular updates on progress through e-mail, a budget forum, or other methods.

Beyond (or in the absence of) an established budget development process, how is information usually gathered on campus? Are there routine or commonly used processes for seeking input? Perhaps the president holds quarterly "state of the university" meetings in which staff and faculty are encouraged to ask questions and offer thoughts. Or the division of student affairs holds monthly all-staff meetings to share ideas from across departments and seek input on strategic planning. Regardless of what mechanisms might or might not be institutionalized, if they exist in some form, they should be seen as inherent vehicles for communication. This is especially true if they foster involvement and collaboration.

Communicating cuts is easier if people have been involved as much as possible in the process. Seeking out the creative ideas of faculty, staff, students, and others is a way to involve others. It also makes communicating the final decision, no matter how difficult, more palatable, because people feel as though they were afforded some voice in the process. In addition, the more people are involved in the discussion, the more likely they are to understand each other's areas, challenges, budgets, and goals and how they relate to institutional mission and priorities. This can change the tenor of communication from "being told" to "being a part of," even if the news is the same.

Richard McKaig, Retired Vice Provost for Student Affairs and Dean of Students, of Indiana University had this to say about conversations on campus about difficult issues:

> It is important to engage in frequent and open conversations about what the problems are and where the money is currently invested. Strategic conversations with directors of the division should be happening well before the budget cut discussion. Talk collectively about strengths, weaknesses, opportunities, and threats. Discuss the division's common goals and which goals have the highest priority. It is important to elevate the conversation above unit levels. It is also important for the directors to gain empathy for their colleagues and a better understanding of the perspectives of each unit. Let them feel each other's pain.

The Importance of Turning to Resources. In the absence of established or healthy institutional processes for dealing with budget cuts or for involving people in decision making, a crisis affords an opportunity to invent or reinvent processes that will serve the institution now and in the future. Highlighting effective processes, even if they have just been "discovered" during the current crisis, can convey that decisions are being made methodically rather than whimsically or spontaneously. In other words, communicating not just the outcome of a process, but the importance and nature of the process itself is an important communication strategy.

Every campus has a unique set of resources to draw on in a time of crisis. Recognizing the power of certain resources, such as informal leaders, institutional data, and established processes, can make the crafting of a communication plan much easier. Using these and other resources affords the opportunity to both strengthen the message and effectively convey it to various stakeholders.

Understanding and Using Available Communication Tools

Resources can be viewed as communication strategies. Typically when referring to communication tools, certain things come to mind: written communication, electronic communication, and in-person communication are three major tools often relied on to convey information. This section explores these tools, looking at each from the standpoint of how to best use them to accomplish certain ends.

While the occasional hard-copy memo still circulates on some campuses, e-mail has become the primary means of written communication at most institutions. Regardless of whether hard copy or electronic, the memo remains the most relied-on method of communication for a number of reasons. When written well, it can convey a substantial amount of information in a consistent format. It also becomes a permanent record of the actions described within it. However, when relied on to outline complex issues, the memo runs the risk of being too general, too overwhelming, confusing, or striking the wrong tone. Several strategies can be employed to reduce these and other risks.

The first is to develop a team approach to memos and messages. Have others as appropriate review memos to get different perspectives and offer thoughts on clarity, focus, and other key elements. The message will become stronger as a result and decrease the likelihood of omissions, confusion, or unintended reactions. Those who are preparing remarks for a speech, the media, or other public speaking opportunities should get feedback on notes, practice delivery in front of a group, and rehearse as much as is necessary to feel comfortable with both content and delivery. At some institutions, presidents and others have staff either write or assist with the writing of speeches, memos, and other forms of communication. Regardless, gathering the appropriate leadership team to review messages before they go out reduces the chance for errors, omissions, and unanticipated consequences while ensuring that key players know the official message and talking points.

A second strategy is to not rely exclusively on written communication. A memo followed by an open forum or town hall meeting allows certain information to get out to everyone and then affords those who want or need it, a time to get clarification and additional information and to ask questions. Using a memo to direct people to the Web for additional details or to the institution's online planning documents allows the written communication to stay focused and brief, while still providing access to additional content and context.

Redundancy is a good thing. Different audiences should get messages in different ways, and key messages should be restated and reinforced with varied communication methods, including representing content visually when possible. A well-placed chart or graph depicting the magnitude of an institution's financial struggles can convey more than a lengthy rationale for why certain positions must be eliminated. Recycling communication created for multiple audiences into press releases is another way to get messages repeated.

When speakers restate their messages, they sharpen their focus and drive home the points they want the audience to remember. Once information is communicated, what do you want people to do with it? You may be communicating about necessary cuts due to budget difficulties, but can you convey this in a way that focuses attention and energy not on the negative but on the positive? For example, suppose an institution is facing $1 million in cuts to balance the budget. This can be placed into a different context by determining how many additional students paying tuition equals $1 million. Furthermore, suppose that one hundred additional students generate $1 million. The message can be shifted to focus on what people can do to enroll those additional students: "If each staff member in the division recruited one more student . . ." The cuts may still need to occur, but as they look ahead, staff and faculty can see that they have at least some control over their future if they focus their efforts away from the negative and toward a meaningful task. This "100 = $1 million" message can be conveyed repeatedly in e-mail, in speeches, at meetings, and elsewhere to create a rallying cry and draw the campus community together. While this is an admittedly simplistic example, it can be translated to other situations unique to any given institution.

Using all available communication methods to reinforce them and reach as many people as possible is the best way to both achieve understanding and appreciation of reality and to reduce the often viral effects of rumors and negativity. If regular updates on the budget are to be held at open forums or meetings across campus, consider videotaping at least one of them. A link to video on the Web page (open to the public or accessed by e-mail password) allows the message to reach those who cannot or choose not to attend in person. It also shows that there is nothing to hide. Newer forms of communication such as Facebook and Twitter may not have a central place in a communication plan, but more and more campuses are finding that social networking sites are an effective way to inform large numbers of students about events, meetings, and information. You might not post information on an institutional Facebook or MySpace page (or Tweet updates about the budget, for that matter), but if these are means by which to reach students and others for activities and events, then they can serve a similar purpose when trying to bolster attendance at a meeting to discuss tuition rates or course cancellations.

E-mails, the Web, public forums, and meetings all play crucial roles in achieving redundant, reliable communication. Another means of communication that should not be overlooked, no matter how unpleasant it is to deliver bad news, is that of in-person communication. One-on-one and small group conversations put a personal face on what may seem to be harsh decisions. They can break down sentiments such as, "The administration has decided . . ." and serve as a reminder that the people who have

NEW DIRECTIONS FOR STUDENT SERVICES • DOI: 10.1002/ss

been charged with making those tough decisions are caring and thoughtful. Blocking out time to walk the halls, visit offices, spend time chatting in the quad, or otherwise be seen talking with staff, students, and faculty can have a huge impact on morale. It can also afford the opportunity to hear rumors firsthand (and dispel them), offer thanks for hard work in difficult circumstances, and acknowledge the fear, pain, or other emotions that are present in tough times.

No matter which mix of communication tools is used to keep the campus community informed, a few additional tools must be employed at all times. Honesty and transparency may be institutional values, but they are also tools. Honest and transparent communication, regardless of how bad the news or whether it is delivered in person or over the Web, will garner trust and confidence.

Timeliness in communication is another tool that can be overlooked. Regular updates, even if there is nothing new to share, can provide a sense of normalcy and comfort. In addition, a regularized communication method provides an opportunity to repeatedly restate key points and messages, ensuring their deeper penetration into the campus psyche.

It can be difficult to stay on message when information is flowing through various forms of written, electronic, and in-person communication. If the institutional chain of command is clear and overarching messages are agreed on, vetted, and communicated clearly at the executive level, they should flow down the command chain and through the various communication tools consistently and appropriately.

Addressing the Different Needs of Various Stakeholders

A communication plan about budget cut decisions should prompt people to reconfirm broad institutional goals, reflect on institutional culture and circumstance, and use institutional resources such as data and the collective thoughts of the community. Communicating about a financial crisis can be an effective rallying cry: "What are we going to do to get through this together while successfully fulfilling our mission?"

Consistency of the message is important, as Marlesa Roney, Vice Provost for Student Success of the University of Kansas, notes: "In most cases, consistent communications, regardless of the constituent group, is best. Otherwise constituent groups can compare communications and interpret varying messages as inconsistent at best, or false and misleading."

It is equally important to be mindful that various stakeholders have different needs and look for those needs to be addressed. Thinking through multiple perspectives might include the following:

- *Students.* Students are likely to be concerned with questions such as: How does this affect me? My degree? My time to degree? My tuition? My professors? Services I use? My overall experience? The student perspective encompasses not only individual student concerns but also how shared governance is practiced and demonstrated on individual campuses. What role does student government play? Fraternities and sororities? The residence hall association? Who are the student opinion leaders? What are the most effective ways for us to communicate with students?

- *Staff.* Staff are likely to focus on questions such as: Am I going to lose my job? Are my colleagues? Will I be taking on more work? How will my students, staff, and operating budget be affected? Is student affairs taking the brunt? What can I do to help? Thinking through staff issues might include these considerations: Are there existing staff groups or councils to use to convey information and/or seek input or ideas? Are there unions or collective bargaining agreements to consider?

- *Parents.* Parent concerns might include: Will costs go up? What will happen to my student's financial aid? What about student employment? Is there help if our family circumstances change? Will my child be able to get her degree? Will the degree be worth as much? How will the services my student uses be affected? Many institutions already have established means of communicating with parents through newsletters, Web sites, listservs, and associations. Does the financial situation warrant a separate outreach to families or inclusion in existing publications? How can upcoming family events be used? Should they? What key role can parents play?

- *Faculty.* Faculty will focus on similar questions as staff—for example, Am I going to lose my job? Are my colleagues? How will my department, research, and travel budget be affected? Faculty often blame the financial crises in higher education on rising administrative costs. While student affairs staff are often concerned about whether they will take the brunt of the cuts, faculty are often perplexed by the growth in noninstructional services. They are also highly concerned about issues of quality. They are concerned with too many students going to college and that administrative pressure to retain students leads to a lowering of standards (Lumina Foundation, 2009).

- *Other administrative colleagues.* It is important to think about other administrative colleagues as well. For example, what is the perspective of the chief financial officer? What is the relationship of the student affairs division with this person? What about the relationship with other executive-level colleagues? How does their perspective not only influence the decision-making process but also how decisions are communicated? Joan Kindle, Vice President of Student Affairs of Harper College, offers this advice: "It is important that before (long before) you find yourself in the budget crunch, you have done a lot of work in helping your executive colleagues understand the importance/critical nature of the work of your areas. When you are in the midst of budget issues with your executive colleagues there is no time to get them to understand the value of your work."

NEW DIRECTIONS FOR STUDENT SERVICES • DOI: 10.1002/ss

- *Community members and the public at large.* Community members may be concerned about the impact of layoffs on the local economy as well as funding impacts on other community agencies, particularly if state or local funds are at issue.

Additional perspectives include those of state higher educational officials as well as college and university presidents themselves. An excellent resource to better understand the challenges, concerns, and multiple perspectives regarding the rising costs of higher education can be found in *Campus Commons: What Faculty, Financial Officers, and Others Think About Controlling College Costs* (2009). This small-scale exploratory study gathered thoughts from chief financial officers from state departments and commissions on higher education, as well as from chief financial officers and faculty from two and four-year public postsecondary institutions, through a series of interviews and focus groups. It offered these key findings:

- Although university presidents believed they had already maximized efficiency, many state and institutional financial officers thought that greater productivity in administrative functions and academic operations was still possible. They believed increasing teaching loads or class size would be a good first step. Faculty, however, were concerned about the whole notion of productivity: "People think that lecturing to 40 students is the same as lecturing to 20 students. Fine, it probably is. But we don't lecture that much anyway. You try grading 40 papers instead of 20 papers," said a faculty member in a focus group session.
- Financial officers were skeptical of the argument that increasing productivity in academic areas will decrease quality and frequently mentioned that distance learning was one way to achieve increased efficiency. Faculty members, however, believed online learning translated into more work for faculty or less learning from students.
- Many state financial officers believed that a good way to increase graduation rates was to financially reward students for completing courses, programs, and degrees rather than rewarding institutions for the number of students enrolled. Faculty viewed this strategy as one that would ultimately increase the number of students with degrees but decrease the actual level of education.

Taking time to understand the multiple perspectives of key stakeholders regarding both the issues and the strategies is foundational to being able to communicate the plan effectively. One method for creating messaging designed to speak directly to different groups' needs or priorities, while sending a consistent message, is through the use of frequently asked questions (FAQs). Although the answers to FAQs will be different for each institution, the FAQ process can be a practical way to adopt a variety of perspectives from myriad constituents and meld them into a set of answerable questions. FAQs can be constructed by asking constituents to submit their questions through online and public forums, or they can be created to help convey a certain perspective.

Public information officers or directors of university and media relations can be essential partners in helping senior student affairs officers think through the issues related to addressing the different needs of various stakeholders.

Also important to consider when addressing a variety of stakeholder perspectives is to think about whether you can share too much information. What is the appropriate line between informing people and confusing them or between attempting to delve into complex issues that leave people with "just enough information to be dangerous" rather than achieving clarity?

Anticipating Reactions and Perpetuating the Message

No matter how much we know about stakeholders and their interests and no matter how many facts we communicate clearly through viable channels, it can be difficult to fully anticipate what reactions will emerge when information is shared. Even after controlling for anticipated pushback, emotional reactions, and variance in the message, concerns can arise that seemingly come out of nowhere. In addition, once action is taken, communicated, and digested and the resulting plans are implemented, what comes next? Ongoing communication will be necessary to respond to the unanticipated and to frame what comes next.

Consider this example of an unanticipated reaction: A division of student affairs needed to eliminate ten staff positions in order to deal with a severe budget shortage. In developing a reduction plan, the institutional strategic plan and divisional five-year plan were used to ensure that any actions would be in line with established priorities. The culture and climate of the campus and the departments to be affected were considered in the formulation of the reduction plan. Directors from various areas were consulted on the impact of one cut versus another, and opportunities for innovation were seized and communicated as a positive outcome of a difficult situation. Once decisions were made, staff whose positions were eliminated were dealt with compassionately, and division-wide meetings were used to communicate the rationale and allow colleagues to process the impending changes. Finally, time was spent fully answering questions from students, faculty, staff, parents, and others through a clear, compelling rationale that was communicated repeatedly. Yet despite all of this work, there was an uproar across the campus after a group of faculty and staff wrote a memo to the president and others about a serious concern. Why? Although every effort was made to focus on the positions that could be eliminated while still protecting student persistence and success, a disproportionate number of those laid off were women over fifty years of age. The memo alleged that this class of employee was being targeted and that the layoffs flew in the face of the stated institutional commitment to affirmative action and equal opportunity. What now?

No matter how much thought goes into a plan or the communication of it, some things can be, and often are, overlooked. Intent can be assumed where there may not have been any. An effective communication plan is prepared to respond appropriately to this type of situation because it will likely arise in some form. In this case, the actions have been taken. There was no intent to target any group or class of employee. The actions taken likely remain the most appropriate for the given circumstances. Responding defensively will probably make matters worse, as will simply ignoring the concerns that were raised. In the end, those who wrote the memo and others may never be satisfied, regardless of what action might be taken.

Even after reactions pop up and are addressed, communication does not end. How do you stay on message about the purpose of the change after the change has occurred? How can you use the change to build a new culture on campus? Can you leverage the change as a springboard or starting point rather than having it seen as an outcome? Did the change actually work? Was it enough to stave off additional cuts? What measures will you use to gauge success? How will you communicate the assessment of outcomes both internally and externally? Can you use your data to make a case for more change if necessary?

These questions can be overlooked as change is implemented. Cuts have been made, people are often now doing more with less, and budget fatigue has made everyone want to think about something else. And yet if data are not collected and sense is not made of the outcomes of the change, the risk is higher that similar problems will arise again. Continuing communication that reminds people why certain decisions were made and what comes next, and shares with them the results of changes as they unfold, can serve to keep constituents focused on strategic plans and make meaning of it all as they move forward. Whether additional cuts become necessary, this ongoing communication has laid the foundation for a better understanding of the issues and a deeper connection to the big picture. If this increased connection to the institution, its values, and its reality can be achieved through ongoing communication, then the crisis that afforded it has not been wasted.

Conclusion

A good communication plan can transform a financial crisis into an opportunity to share the legacy of the institution or division. What is important, how did we get here, and where are going? It can serve as a rallying cry to bring people together as strategic priorities and missions are reaffirmed.

A good communication strategy is clear and consistent about when a decision has been made and when input is still being collected and considered. It is also helpful to:

- Identify timelines
- Recognize and appreciate the feedback process used
- Communicate empathy for losses
- Reiterate that decisions have been difficult
- Remind people why decisions were made
- Outline next steps
- Share the results of the strategies implemented

The last point cannot be overemphasized. Sharing the effectiveness of strategies can help heal loss, build community, and effectively move on.

A budget crisis is an emotional event that is personal and encompasses many perspectives, priorities, and programs. It also creates key opportunities to revisit an institution's values, priorities, relationships, and mission.

Reference

Lumina Foundation. *Campus Commons: What Faculty, Financial Officers and Others Think About Controlling College Costs.* New York: Lumina Foundation, 2009.

JONATHAN ELDRIDGE *is the vice president for student affairs at Southern Oregon University.*

TISA MASON *is the vice president for student affairs at Fort Hayes State University in Kansas.*

NEW DIRECTIONS FOR STUDENT SERVICES • DOI: 10.1002/ss

5

This chapter reports on a qualitative study conducted in 2005 and 2009, describing the experiences of twelve senior student affairs officers at public universities as they managed significant budget reductions.

The New Normal: Senior Student Affairs Officers Speak Out About Budget Cutting

C. Renee Romano, Jan Hanish, Calvin Phillips, Michael D. Waggoner

"This is not an easy time to be a budget officer or financial manager in an institution of higher education" (Schuh, 2000, p. 73). Written at the beginning of the twenty-first century, those words seem prophetic as we approach the end of the century's first decade. In the opening years of the century, federal and state governments, feeling financially flush from the economic boom of the 1990s, enacted massive tax cuts. At the same time, a downturn in the world economy rippled through the United States, ending a sustained period of record economic growth. The combined effect of these two trends was to immediately and dramatically reduce tax revenues and future revenue projections. In late 2008 and early 2009, the economy took a nearly unprecedented downturn, plunging the country into a deep recession. State legislatures scrambled to implement budget cuts, including midyear rescissions, throughout all aspects of the public sector, including higher education.

To understand the experiences of leaders in student affairs in higher education and to document the strategies they used to cut budgets and the results of these actions, we conducted a qualitative research study using public institutions as case studies. Data were gathered in 2005 through phone interviews with senior student affairs officers (SSAOs) from twelve public colleges and universities to study the budget reductions that had occurred in the previous three to four years. After the recession hit in 2009,

the researchers gathered additional data from the same institutions to determine if budget cuts were still a factor and if the strategies the SSAOs used and the results had changed over the ensuing four years. Several research questions were probed in both stages of the process: How have student affairs organizations used reduction, downsizing, and integration of units to respond to budget reductions? Did these factors change over time? What are the resulting changes in organizational structure, services, people, and organizational culture? How were student affairs staff and leaders affected as a result of budget cuts? In the context of budget reductions and strategies, what do SSAOs see as future financial issues in the profession?

Participant responses revealed how SSAOs dealt with persistent budget reductions over an eight-year period, the impact of decisions, and ongoing challenges to their leadership. The results are reported describing strategies the SSAOs used to reduce spending and increase income, the outcomes of budget cutting as perceived by the SSAOs, and the leadership qualities and skills they relied on when making these difficult decisions. Finally, the researchers developed critical lessons learned that may be considered as SSAOs and other student affairs staff are challenged in the coming years with what is anticipated to be lingering budget challenges.

Methodology of the Study

Twelve state-supported institutions from across the United States were selected for the study from an analysis of five years of state appropriations to higher education from 1999 to 2004 (Armone, 2004). Institutions sustaining significant cuts were identified using the criteria of at least 3 to 4 percent annual reductions for three or more years during this period. Regional representation was also sought within the criteria. Four institutions were selected in each of three size categories: large (enrollment greater than 20,000), medium (10,000 to 19,999), and small (fewer than 10,000). In 2005, phone interviews were conducted with the SSAOs of these institutions. All interviews were transcribed and analyzed for themes relating to the research questions.

In 2009, the SSAOs from the same institutions were contacted again to revisit the research questions, determine if budget reductions were still a factor, and assess how their strategies and results had changed. The researchers were successful in conducting follow-up interviews with eight of the twelve institutions in the original research. Participants in the second phase of the research were given summaries of the first interview in order to allow them to review the content prior to the second interview. These interviews were then reviewed and analyzed for overall themes, including any changes noted between 2005 and 2009. Several important themes emerged, including strategies the SSAOs used to reduce expenses or increase income, the results they observed, the effects of the cuts on them and their staff, and the leadership skills and qualities they demonstrated throughout the difficult process of budget cutting.

NEW DIRECTIONS FOR STUDENT SERVICES • DOI: 10.1002/ss

In 2005, the SSAOs had been cutting budgets for the previous three or four years and had developed processes to make critical decisions and manage change in their organizations. These included communicating with and empowering staff and managing the needs of staff and students in new, creative ways. They emphasized the importance of modeling behavior and demonstrating a sense of optimism for the future. They also talked about increased levels of stress they experienced as a result. These administrators experienced budget cuts for several consecutive years, not knowing when or if a recovery would take place.

In 2009, the second round of interviews revealed that cuts were still occurring and the strategies they discussed in 2005 were continued or slightly altered. Several reported a period of leveling off or slight increases in dollars after 2005, but the recession of 2008 and 2009 created serious restrictions in state allocations to the universities. Others reported a continuous period of budget cuts over the period between the original interview in 2005 and the second interviews in 2009.

Although the SSAOs still used many of the same processes and strategies in 2009, they found that they were rethinking approaches such as extensive communication, assessment, and fundraising. They found a strong need to be able to explain the value of student affairs to other administrators, faculty, parents, and the public. These themes are explored in this chapter. Because of the similarities between 2005 and 2009, the results are woven together in this chapter, and differences are illustrated. The words of the respondents illustrate the authentic experiences of the SSAOs so that we may fully understand the context of student affairs leadership at these institutions.

The Process of Cutting Budgets

Although the ways that the states imposed the revenue reductions on the institutions varied, the process of reducing revenue adopted by the SSAOs in both 2005 and 2009 were remarkably similar. They relied on clear and consistent communication with staff and revisited student affairs mission and goals as a way to guide their decision making.

Communication. In all cases and in both time periods, SSAOs talked about the fact that they spent a lot of time communicating with staff throughout the organization. One vice president said, "We kept staff involved in what we were doing. I didn't do anything in isolation, didn't do anything in secret. I didn't dream anything up." Conscientious, effective communication not only facilitated the work of budget reduction, it also helped manage the consequences for staff morale. In addition, sharing information was one of the ways that trust was developed among staff, and trust enabled the organization to continue functioning effectively.

During the second round of interviews in 2009, communication was still important, but one respondent mentioned that she believed the staff just wanted her to tell them what to do without a lot of discussion. There

NEW DIRECTIONS FOR STUDENT SERVICES • DOI: 10.1002/ss

was a sense of trying to balance the desire and commitment to transparency and open communication with the fact that the situation was evolving almost daily. Another respondent from a Midsized midwestern university said he tried to find a balance between having conversations, getting information about next year's budget, and simply informing people. He explained, "They say, `Just tell me what to do and I'll do it.'"

Clarity on Values and Mission. By and large, agreement over values sets the tone for the process. One vice president from a medium-sized institution in the Midwest said that his staff agreed to be honest and support one another. Discussions at another midsized institution of potential scenarios of cuts from 15 to 25 percent in 2009 began at a staff retreat to discuss the division's core values. The retreat was followed by a series of university-wide forums that included students to determine what was necessary and what was fluff about the institutional programs and services. In addition to clarifying values, institutions developed a range of strategies to achieve their respective resource objectives.

Strategies. With respect to strategies used to cut budgets, the SSAOs discussed personnel and salaries, job eliminations and reorganizations, professional development, technology, student employment, graduate assistantships, privatization, auxiliary services, and student fees, grants, fundraising, and assessment.

Salaries. For the most part, staff salaries were not reduced, but at some institutions, salary increases were not provided for a period of time. A vice president of a large Midwestern university explained that if they lost a staff member and did not rehire, they used that salary line to increase the salaries of staff who remained. SSAOs were concerned that reducing or not increasing salaries would have a negative effect on morale and were concerned about the possibility of losing good personnel and the ability to attract good people in the future.

Reorganization and Position Eliminations. Senior student affairs officers in this study tried to protect staff, which they considered their most valuable resource, but they often looked to reassignments or reorganization to meet the required cuts. The vice president at a medium-sized university in the Northeast explained, "The strategy was to protect those who are here, consolidate and reassign, and fill where there are vacancies with existing personnel."

Retirements and resignations provided cost saving opportunities for the institutions, although they sometimes decimated the units in which they occurred. Many of the responding institutions chose to seize the moment to achieve new organizational objectives by looking at the structure of their organizations, combining positions or departments. There were efforts to work closely with academic affairs, and in some cases, this meant combining resources to support positions or programs on either side. This was demonstrated by a small mid-Atlantic university as follows: "We eliminated a job, our director of career services, and combined and collapsed that office with cooperative education, which was in the academic affairs here. That merged into the student affairs area. With that office merger, there was a net loss of two positions."

Another SSAO at a large university in the East was proud of the reorganizations that occurred as a result of restrictions in resources. His organization created an integrated service center, combining enrollment services, the registrar's office, and veterans' services. He believed this reorganization improved efficiency and service to students.

Professional Development. Most SSAOs expressed the importance of professional development since travel seemed to be first on the chopping block, and they understood that budget cuts had a negative impact on the professional development of their staff. Because of the lack of monies to send personnel to professional development activities off-campus, some of the institutions brought workshops and presentations to the campus as a way to make sure that professional development was not neglected.

Technology. The use of technology was a major strategy in some institutions to help where the shortage of staff was an issue. Many decided to invest monies in technology that supported services to students. Technology provided more access to services to students who were familiar with and relied on computers for information. SSAOs reported that the students in fact were more satisfied with online methods of service delivery and perceived online services to be more efficient.

Student Employment and Graduate Assistantships. The use of student employment was a strategy several institutions used to help with the shortage of staff in offices. Several institutions felt the need to support students by employing them, especially since rises in tuition caused financial hardships. It was also clear that student employees were being asked to do more and that the number of students working in these offices increased. However, the presence of labor unions on some campuses complicated the movement from full-time support staff to students because union leaders at a couple of universities viewed losses in full-time jobs replaced by student workers as a threat to their members.

Graduate assistantships were reduced at some institutions and increased at others depending on the circumstances. The vice president of a small mid-Atlantic institution said that he was more dependent on graduate assistantships than in the past, for which he received a grant from the College Board of Historically Black Colleges.

Outsourcing. The findings of this study indicated that the majority of the institutions decided that the use of outsourcing was not the best course of action in dealing with the budget cuts. The respondent from a medium-sized mid-Atlantic university said, "One of the things that our experience here has taught us is that privatization and outsourcing really doesn't save you anything most times, and then if you don't get what you want out of it, you end up having to pay a high price from the other end to build your new infrastructure again." However, two respondents determined that outsourcing was a necessity in specific circumstances to provide additional income. The administrator of a medium-sized university in the Northeast indicated that outsourcing with a company to provide testing services had positive results. Another SSAO from a large Southeastern institution outsourced the bookstore and believed that was a good decision for it.

Auxiliary Services. The one area that the majority of the institutions described as a benefit through the cuts was supporting nonauxiliary areas in student affairs with auxiliary dollars. It was common practice to move appropriate personnel from state funds to auxiliary fund sources. The administrator of a large Midwestern institution described his situation: "So when things got tight, I made it clear that they [auxiliaries] were in the best position to help the rest of their colleagues as we faced these difficult times. So, we did things like, when we cut a position that was on state funding, one of the auxiliaries would pick that position up."

In addition to supporting positions, auxiliary services provided funds to support the budget cuts in other ways, such as supporting programs through food services, waiving rental fees, and providing additional staffing for events.

In the 2009 interviews, one SSAO at a midsized institution in the East commented that the spirit had changed and her institution was more accepting of how auxiliary funds could be used to support activities that contributed to the overall student experience. She stated, "One difference now is that people recognize that student fees and designated funds are places we have to go to preserve the core." She perceived this as a very different philosophy from the late 1990s or early 2000s.

Student Fees. Many of the institutions in this study expressed that decreases in state support have left them no choice but to make up the difference by increasing fees or developing new fees to support services in their area. One respondent talked about raising the transcript and graduation fees and implementing an application fee that raised three-quarters of a million dollars annually.

In 2009 during a period of recession when families were struggling financially, there was more desire to keep tuition and fee increases to a minimum than during the budget cuts recorded in 2005. The tendency to look to fees as a way to manage budget difficulties was offset by the awareness of issues of access and affordability for students.

Grants. Some institutions considered grant funding as a way to generate additional revenue, but for the most part, grants were not a great resource for providing the financial means needed to support the budget cuts. The exceptions to this general response to grant funding were the historically black institutions that reported receiving Title IIIB grant monies from the federal government. The perception of the SSAOs at these institutions was that these funds were vital to the survival of their student services.

Fundraising. Fundraising consistently emerged as an income-generating strategy. In 2005, it was evident that student affairs organizations were engaged in developing an internal structure to support fundraising. A few administrators felt that this placed them in competition with existing fundraising activities, but this response was the exception. Most vice presidents reported that they were in one stage of fundraising activity or another: they were considering it, beginning new efforts, or had been involved in development for a while. In the second round of interviews in 2009, fundraising was a much stronger, more developed strategy to increasing income.

Assessment. Assessment as a way to determine what programs and services were more or less important was mentioned in 2005 and became more prominent by 2009. In the 2009 interviews, several SSAOs indicated that assessment was more critical than it had been previously, both to determine where funding should go as well as to justify programs and services to others. One respondent explained, "Since 2005 I've put into place an assessment piece to answer the questions: What, so what, and then what? Every department is doing at least one assessment whether it is student satisfaction, needs assessment or learning outcomes. That will help us redirect money."

Perceived Outcomes of Budget Cutting

The strategies we just noted came through consistently in our interviews with SSAOs, but the methods had consequences. Some of the outcomes were anticipated, but others were unexpected.

After cutting budgets for several consecutive years, the SSAOs had a chance to reflect on the outcomes of budget cutting and a number of strategies that rose to the level of best practices. From their perspectives, one of the most positive outcomes of budget cutting was the reexamination of values and purposes of student affairs divisions.

In addition, respondents indicated that the process of cutting budgets forced them to look for greater efficiencies within their operations. In order to maintain their core principles and deal with reduced budgets, administrators looked for efficiencies and found them in the way of reorganization, interdepartmental cooperation, and increased use of technology. A respondent from a small Southeastern institution said, "One of the ripple effects of having to review your resources is that everything is supposed to be more efficient, and it also encourages people to be much more creative and imaginative in our programs and services they offer. I think people have become much more attuned to the need to collaborate across lines."

Several respondents discussed how the outcome of cuts and reorganization was a greater reliance on relationships built within the university. This included collaboration within student affairs departments and with academics as well.

It was not unusual for the SSAOs in the study to express concern about how budget tensions affected staff, their careers, salaries, and productivity. As disconcerting as the personal effect on current staff was, some believed that limited salaries could affect the ability to be competitive in hiring in the future.

In addition to these outcomes of budget cutting, SSAOs found that they did their jobs differently in several ways.

Leadership in Tough Times

In the interviews, many SSAOs spoke to the leadership qualities and skills they relied on during these challenging times. Processes that emphasized teamwork and collaboration were essential, and respondents talked extensively about keeping morale up and employees motivated. Several individuals noted the need to stay optimistic with their staff and model a positive attitude. One individual said, "The hardest part of the last four years has been trying to maintain the morale and give people hope when they did not have all the tools that they needed to do their job." The SSAO of a large university in the Midwest said that during this time, he realized how important symbolism was with respect to what he attended and how he acted: "When you're in difficult times, folks are looking for an anchor. They want somebody solid that they know is going to advocate for them and will take some risk with them but also help them be creative and be a cheerleader. They deserve that, in my estimation."

Years of cutting budgets had a deep personal effect on SSAOs at these public universities. Some administrators were tired and discouraged from dealing with the budget cuts. Several talked about working longer hours and having additional staff reporting directly to them. Another individual said, "It's increased my stress level about tenfold."

Others were energized by the situation. One in particular who had previous experience in development was able to maximize fundraising during this time and used his experience to make the best of a bad situation: "I felt like this was such a challenge. I loved it. It was because I had good mentoring myself and good experience that I was able to survive this."

Dealing with budget cuts and the desire to maintain quality service to students as well as support to staff clearly caused a great deal of personal stress for those expected to manage the situation. Each SSAO interviewed referred to the worry and anxiety over the effects that budget reductions had personally on both students and staff, as well as on the programs and services provided by their respective departments. The vice president of student affairs at a medium-sized university in the Northeast said, "It is only human nature to feel diminished, devalued, marginalized, isolated, and so on. I don't like to use the word *depression*, but more a real sense of a gloom and doom kind of milieu, and then moments of optimism. And then almost I can recall everyone feeling as though they were numb from it all, from the intensity, university wide and within the division." Another respondent said, "It was a painful process. In the moment, throughout the moments, there were those times when you just had to ask yourself, 'Are you doing the right thing?'"

Whether discouraged, stressed, or energized, most of the administrators expressed a sense of hope and optimism for the future. Others realized that although they had always been called on to be articulate about describing the value of student affairs to the academic mission of the institution, it became even more critical during this time. For example, one individual from a small public liberal arts institution said, "I think it is our job as educators and perhaps even more our job as student affairs professionals to advocate for the value, the educational and societal value, of a traditional college experience." Several respondents addressed the change in the position of public higher education, the need to communicate our value to citizens of the state and to be cognizant that funding is no longer automatic.

The SSAO of a historically black university mentioned the need to communicate "the connection between student development and having access to resources." When speaking to churches, civic groups, and professional associations, this individual was mindful about including information about the needs of the university and the students.

The SSAO at one large Midwestern university reported in 2009 that the university president created a new resource management model that required him to present his financial needs to a university committee chaired by an academic administrator. This SSAO was required to fully educate the committee about student affairs programs and services and was gratified to see great appreciation for student affairs from his academic colleagues.

Lessons Learned

The words and experiences of these student affairs administrators led to several important lessons learned for moving into uncertain territory. Modeling the way or "walking the walk," or however else this is described, is an important leadership trait demonstrated by the SSAOs in this study who talked about the importance of modeling behavior. They did not travel as much when their staff travel was restricted. They gave up resources, increased the number of people reporting to them, reorganized to create greater efficiencies, and felt the results of greater stress. The SSAOs were aware not only of what they said but, much more important, what they did.

Another lesson learned is the act of inspiring staff through difficult times. Maintaining a positive and optimistic attitude was essential to managing these difficult times: "The climb to the top is arduous and long. People become exhausted, frustrated, and disenchanted. They are often tempted to give up. Leaders must *encourage the heart* of their followers to carry on" (Kouzes and Posner, 1987, p. 13). Indeed in this case the "arduous climb to the top" is the route of navigating murky budget waters. SSAO leadership provided the inspiration to keep going regardless of the length and duration of the climb.

In 2009, the SSAOs reported that year after year of trying to manage limited and reduced resources resulted in budget fatigue. Staff reached a point where they felt they were being asked to look for options when none existed. One SSAO described staff as simply wanting direction, wanting to be told what to do, and then they would find the way to do it.

So while inclusion and communication are important strategies, the SSAO must know how to balance an inclusive process with the hard reality that some staff are not always comfortable or prepared to make difficult budget decisions. This balance between complete transparency and filtering is complex, and perhaps one of the most important leadership qualities for leaders in higher education. This understanding is an organically developed skill that grows from well-balanced leaders who have developed authentic relationships with staff.

In addition, the heavy reliance on fee-generated dollars can complicate staff relationships. Furloughs, hiring freezes, and pay freezes are all being used on college campuses to respond to budget crises. Staff funded with state dollars might look to staff in other funding streams that are not held to the same approach and wonder why such issues do not affect their colleagues. These complications can be mitigated with extensive and clear communication, but not without negative effects on staff morale. From the perspective of the public, and in particular students and parents, the differences among state dollars, tuition, auxiliaries, fees, and development funds are a mystery. Students and their families are paying more and more for a college education, and as the vice president of a large university in the East said, "They don't want to hear us bellyaching about budget cuts."

Finally, budgeting processes and models are intensifying the need for student affairs leaders to describe and justify the value of their programs and services to those outside student affairs, particularly in academic affairs. The competition for scarce resources requires everyone to assess, revise, and be accountable to quality and value added to the educational experience. The need for assessment, particularly on learning outcomes in the out-of-class environment, is even more critical than in the past. In addition, the need to have collaborative partnerships with academic affairs and others across the university is intensified. If student affairs could ever afford to function independently, those days are long gone. The learning environment has benefited from partnerships with academics, and now the economic environment demands it for our very survival.

Concerns for the Future

This study revealed several potentially long-term consequences in the decisions that are being made in higher education and specifically in student affairs. One area of concern is the shift of budgets to auxiliary or fee support. Respondents in this study believe that these times of limited resources are going to continue, perhaps indefinitely. The levels of state support to higher education may never completely rebound. Since these budget cuts are not short term as they may have been in the past, SSAOs need to think about the effects of shifting sources of income. SSAOs talked about increasing pressure on auxiliaries to shoulder the burden of budget cuts, and often good arguments are made to support such actions. But data suggest that student loan debt continues to rise. In 2008, the College Board reported that the total educational loans more than doubled from $41 billion (in 2007 dollars) in 1997–98 to $85 billion in 2007–08. ("Trends in Student Aid," 2008). Affordability of higher education already challenges access for many students and their families. Shifting costs to auxiliaries and fees may solve some internal budget issues, but the result will still be increasing costs to students. However new funds are generated, taking into consideration issues of access and affordability must be at the forefront of these decisions.

Technology has provided some solutions in managing budget cuts, as some departments relied on Web-based services to meet the needs of students. Technologically savvy students welcome more efficient technology, more services on the Web, and so on. However, this approach is more applicable in some areas than others, and we must be vigilant about the long-term effects of the loss of student contact with staff from the perspective of both students and staff. An awareness of which services need to stay high touch and which can be addressed through the high-tech approach is needed. Just because a service or program can be delivered through the use of technology, the question should always be asked whether it should be delivered in this fashion. Perhaps additional research is needed to determine the quality of service to students delivered online and in person.

This study also has provided information to suggest that staff retirements or resignations can be seen as a means of dealing with budget cuts. However, as seasoned staff move on and are not replaced, the wisdom, experience, and expertise they have cultivated over the years leave with them. Young professionals have not had the time to develop their skill sets, and professional development is an easy target for budget cuts. How will these young professionals learn the nuances of the profession and develop deeper understanding and broader skill sets if they have neither the benefit of experienced mentors nor opportunities for staff development? Student affairs could experience a loss of professional wisdom and experience that will be difficult to replace. There are serious long-term consequences to the staff decisions that seem to offer short-term budget solutions. It is incumbent on student affairs administrators to give serious consideration to how these staff decisions can affect not only the institution and its students, but the profession as a whole.

Conclusion

The respondents recognized the difficulties of dealing with deep and sustained budget cuts. They focused their energies on managing cuts through increased efficiency and creativity. The effects on staff and programs were sometimes negative, but those interviewed in this study always came back to the good that came of the difficult process: reflective analysis of mission, creative solutions, improved relationships and partnerships, and enhanced service through technology.

They also realized that cutting budgets is something that we will be dealing with on a regular basis into the future. What used to be a cyclical or occasional experience is now becoming "the new normal," as one SSAO described it. This leader from the Southeast asked, "What will be the new normal for higher education? We used to plan on things to get through the rough periods for one, two, or three years. Now the question is, What if this is the good time? What will be the new normal, and what will we, employees, and students adjust to?" Another SSAO called for change in student affairs preparatory programs to put more emphasis on budget, organizational change, and change management.

These actions uphold Rhatigan's (2000) assessment of student affairs practitioners: "Practitioners do not enjoy the luxury of certainty. It is profoundly true that student affairs administrators must often proceed without knowing exactly what they are doing. We either act or step aside. This requires judgment and faith, the willingness to be vulnerable and to take risks" (p. 22).

The challenges of cutting budgets are testing student affairs leaders. Their values, care for students and one another, communication skills, compassion, flexibility, and creativity have served them and their institutions well in these difficult times.

References

Arnone, M. "State Spending on Colleges Drops for the First Time in 11 years." Chronicle of Higher Education, January 16, 2004.

Kouzes, J. M. and Posner, B. Z. *The Leadership Challenge: How to Get Extraordinary Things Done in Organizations*. San Francisco: Jossey-Bass, 1987.

Palmer, J.C. (January 16, 2004), Fact File: State Appropriations for Higher Education, Chronicle of Higher Education.

Rhatigan, J. J. "The History and Philosophy of Student Affairs." In M. J. Barr, M. K. Desler, and Associates (eds.), *The Handbook of Student Affairs Administration*. (2nd ed.) San Francisco: Jossey-Bass, 2000.

Schuh, J. H. "Fiscal Pressures on Higher Education and Student Affairs." In M. J. Barr, M. K. Desler, and Associates (eds.), *The Handbook of Student Affairs Administration*. (2nd ed.) San Francisco: Jossey-Bass, 2000.

"Trends in Student Aid." 2008. Retrieved July 26, 2009, from http://professionals.collegeboard.com/profdownload/trends-in-student-aid-2008.pdf

C. RENEE ROMANO *is the vice chancellor for student affairs at the University of Illinois, Urbana-Champaign.*

JAN HANISH *is the assistant vice president for outreach and special programs at the University of Northern Iowa.*

CALVIN PHILLIPS *is the associate vice president and dean of students at the University of Texas Pan American.*

MICHAEL D. WAGGONER *is a professor of educational leadership, counseling, and postsecondary education at the University of Northern Iowa.*

NEW DIRECTIONS FOR STUDENT SERVICES • DOI: 10.1002/ss

6

This chapter offers a case study of how one institution has implemented budget reductions. Using a narrative approach, the vice president for student life reviews the issues faced and the processes used to implement the changes.

Preserving the Future from the Demands of the Present

Frank P. Ardaiolo

As Winthrop University's 2008–09 academic year started, executive officers (the president plus the five vice presidents) and three assistants to the president sequestered ourselves for a six-day planning and budget meeting to address the challenges at hand. We were facing an imminent $735,000 reduction to our annual state appropriation. University president Anthony J. DiGiorgio, a realist who rarely catastrophizes problems that can be creatively solved, seemed to be unusually pessimistic about the state budget and its ongoing ability to support state-funded universities. Although the president's warning and predictions rang clearly, most of us on the leadership team hoped that things couldn't get worse, trusting that further reductions would be unrealized. Unfortunately, in this case, the president's perception was accurate: the budget worsened, and with its deterioration came drastic reductions to South Carolina's public higher education.

As the 2008–09 fiscal year unfolded, Winthrop lost $8 million in state support. The institution coped with these rescissions by cutting services, reprioritizing commitments, and implementing (as a last resort) a nine-day employee furlough. Although the furlough decision was difficult, it protected students from a seven hundred dollar semester increase in tuition that otherwise would have been imposed. But even with these strategies in place, it was clear that salary cuts and program reductions would be implemented since the $8 million state reduction was not being restored. Adding to the strain of the state budget was Governor Mark Sanford's refusal to accept the federal State Fiscal Stabilization Funds ($3.1 million for Winthrop) until

New Directions for Student Services, no. 129, Spring 2010 © Wiley Periodicals, Inc.
Published online in Wiley InterScience (www.interscience.wiley.com) • DOI: 10.1002/ss.352

he was forced to do so by a state supreme court ruling in late June 2009. Amid the challenge, Winthrop's leadership team reconfirmed its commitment to maintaining the identity it had forged and to actualizing the institution's core values, governing principles, and ground rules that would direct the content and process of the decision making that lay ahead.

Honing the Tools That Guided the Decision-Making Process

Facilitating budget decisions in challenging economic times is no easy task. Before any deliberations even occurred, the president and his executive team developed a set of tools that would frame both the process and content of this decision making. Along with the university's articulated institutional identity, we used three sets of tools as we moved forward. The first set, a core values and commitment one, was derived from the annual "Visions of Distinction 2009–10" document. The second set encompassed three governing principles that the president fashioned from the core values. In the third set of tools were the explicit ground rules that would direct the processes we were about to initiate.

Institutional Identity. Winthrop is a comprehensive public university that provides personalized undergraduate, graduate, and continuing education programs to sixty-five hundred students. Forty of its bachelor's, master's, and specialist degrees are nationally accredited by their respective disciplinary associations, reflecting the university's commitment to be among the top institutions of its kind. The campus houses twenty-four hundred students, and it expects all undergraduates to live on campus their first two years.

Core Values. The annual planning document, "Visions of Distinction," highlights the university's core values—a value set that overtly framed budget conversations and the decisions that emerged from them. The following commitment statements found on page 2 of the document reflect those core values:

- We center the Winthrop experience on student development inspired by our commitment to the liberal arts traditions, to national-caliber professional education, and to developing leadership and civic responsibility;
- We nurture collective and individual growth, enlightenment, and transformation;
- We value the search for truth through reasoned and disciplined inquiry, innovation, and free expression;
- We embrace multiculturalism and the broadest possible diversity of people and perspectives;
- We share a strong sense of place—a beautiful, historic campus with a collegial and caring atmosphere; and

NEW DIRECTIONS FOR STUDENT SERVICES • DOI: 10.1002/ss

- We fulfill and enhance the nature and character of the university through policies and resources that reflect and advance these ideals and aspirations.

Governing Principles. The core values and commitment statements helped the president formulate three succinct principles that would directly guide the upcoming reduction exercise: protecting the quality of students' Winthrop experiences, protecting the safety and security of the campus, and continuing to recruit a student body reflective of the nature and character of Winthrop.

Ground Rules. It was soon clear that the emerging content or product of the budget reduction exercises would reflect the university's core values and principles. While the substance of the decision making was being shaped by values and principles, the decision-making process was being framed by a set of explicit ground rules. From the start, the president and the cabinet designed the following set of ground rules and agreed that the entire budget process would adhere strictly to these rules (Ardaiolo, 2009):

All university activities and programs were subject to scrutiny. There were to be no sacred projects, programs, or functions immune from discussion, examination, and potential modification, reduction, or elimination.

All discussions were to be conducted in the strictest confidence. None other than the nine at the table would be engaged in this level of discussion, and we were expected to cease conversations at the conclusion of the meetings.

We were to check our professional and personal egos at the door. We were expected to serve as a high functioning team that transcended departmental responsibilities.

We were to address and quickly recover from any type of professional depression that we had heretofore experienced. Our charge as executive leaders was to maintain and exude a positive morale while imparting some sense of confidence to our staffs.

We were to formulate and share uniform responses to anticipated concerns or questions posed by any members of our academic community. We needed to coordinate communication, ensuring that constituents and stakeholders were informed in accurate and on-going ways. Written and oral messages would communicate a realistic and, to the extent possible, positive perspective.

We were to solicit suggestions from all campus constituents. We actively encouraged people to use a newly developed Web-based response system to post questions and to stay informed.

We were to be hard-minded yet fair. We were expected to use our creative and critical thinking skills and to maintain a "can-do" problem-solving mentality.

We held primacy in decision making. When necessary, we were to gently remind questioning or skeptical university members that administrators

NEW DIRECTIONS FOR STUDENT SERVICES • DOI: 10.1002/ss

have primacy for managing and reaching budgetary decisions; faculty have primacy for determining instructional matters. We were expected to use the faculty governance structures that are meant to facilitate dialogue between faculty and administrators.

Revisiting Our Identity: Maintaining Academic Excellence

Winthrop's identity is tied to academic excellence and being known as a top-notch comprehensive university. Aligned with that priority, we decided first to identify nonclassroom expenditures that we could reduce or eliminate. The following list delineates some of the specific reductions in this area:

• Cancelling, combining, or using Web-based replacement publications to trim costs
• Managing (not canceling) all professional travel, with trips involving students who were making presentations to professional conferences given first priority
• Deferring an arts festival
• Cancelling Winthrop cosponsorship and other costs related to an annual regional wellness event
• Holding a number of staff vacancies open and redistributing the work from those positions among other employees
• Delaying rotation of new computer replacements to four years from three years
• Delaying acquisition of the next phase of replacement vehicles for the university maintenance and police fleet
• Limiting hours of operation for some university facilities

The New Reality

Using the ground rules to shape the budget reductions process and the tools and values to shape the outcomes, Winthrop was well positioned to face its future, even the challenging one that lay ahead.

A Key Relationship with Academic Affairs. Winthrop's Division of Student Life has a long-standing mission statement directly aligned with the vision and mission of the university:

> The Division of Student Life provides opportunities and services to foster student development along cognitive, personal, and interpersonal dimensions. As educators, we work with our faculty colleagues to nurture and stimulate student learning and success within a pluralistic campus community. We accomplish this by delivering primary services that provide for the out-of-classroom caring for students, the foundation upon which classroom growth occurs [Winthrop University, Division of Student Life, 2009].

Through the annual planning, assessment, and professional development of student life staff, the division has been integral to the university's recent successes. Student life staff are considered partners with faculty colleagues in helping the university operationalize its mores, nature, and character, that is, its core values. Many of the professional student life staff are involved with Winthrop's University College, whose "purpose is to increase and enhance student achievement, responsibility, and engagement throughout the Winthrop Experience . . . University College coordinates curricular and co-curricular programs enabling faculty and staff to work across disciplines. This type of collaboration ensures that every Winthrop student, regardless of his or her ultimate degree goal, has a common academic foundation and a commitment to lifelong learning, leadership, and service" (Winthrop University, 2009). My awareness of and appreciation for academic affairs and other administrative divisions was key to participating in global discussions. I had been at the decision-making table for many years and was well positioned to shape the decisions that would help us resolve the most difficult budget situation to arise in forty years. My biggest challenge was to do right by my institution while not allowing disproportionate cuts to dramatically impair student service–related activities. This was an important task since student affairs is often an easy target when chief executives and academic administrators are prone to protect instructors and seek the line of least resistance.

By keeping a broad understanding of student learning front and center, we went deeper than just focusing solely on teaching and faculty rewards in our discussions. We also discussed types of facilities that promote in- and out-of-class learning and overall student interest and concerns. These conversations were framed by a rational budget reduction decision-making model that constantly revisited the institutional mission.

The Real Thing. Our first critical session began the first week of December 2008. The members of the leadership team were somber because preliminary analysis showed we were probably going to face a 50 percent cut of our state appropriation. The first item the president placed on the proverbial budget axe table were the seven full-time positions recently added to our residence life staff. My response to this suggestion was, "Yes, sir, it's appropriate given the times to examine this." The appropriate tone had been set for all.

For eighteen years, student life had advocated for the hiring of full-time residence hall directors in seven of our buildings. During that time, the halls had been at or over capacity, and a student majority reported satisfaction. Rather than spend funds on hiring these seven full-time resident directors, available resources were used to remodel the halls and complete other projects that directly benefited our residents. During this same period, the halls were managed by graduate assistants. Finally, three years ago, we were allowed to hire two professional residential learning coordinators to help create "academic success communities." By 2008–09, we finally had a master's-level-trained residence life professional in each our seven halls, and the overall program is showing even higher marks in student learning, satisfaction, and retention.

Still, the confidential list for possible cutbacks and changes began to grow. In considering this list, the president presented a categorical schema to outline all we could examine for cutting back our overall institutional budget:

- Salary containment or reduction
- Eliminate, redesign, or defer programs
- Nonsalary containment or reduction
- New revenue opportunities

He reminded us to see each potential reduction item through the tripartite lens of protecting the quality of students' Winthrop experiences in and out of the classroom, protecting the safety and security of the campus, and continuing recent initiatives to recruit a student body.

As the budget crisis worsened, you could almost hear protective sentiments being voiced: "My responsibilities [my program, my discipline] are more important than others! Cut over there, not here!" As anxiety increased, we continued to post all suggestions for budget savings or cuts.

The president repeatedly reminded us that our real responsibility was to preserve the institution's future from the demands of the present. We could not cut some things the less informed might suggest, no matter how well intentioned, for they may not understand their immediate cost-benefit returns or their significance for long-term sustainability. Furthermore, we needed to act quickly. There was no time to engage in widespread analysis or to conduct open forums that might pit well-meaning staff or faculty groups against each other or the administration.

Meeting Personally the Task at Hand. Facing my own trepidations about the budget, I used the solitude afforded by our semester break to analyze some of the options I was asked to consider. In considering these options, I did something I had not done for awhile: I spent two days reviewing every line item for the eighty institutional budgets, totaling $10 million, in the Division of Student Life. This overdue self-induced exercise triggered valuable introspection, allowing me to examine and resolve certain dissonances. It also enforced a renewed sense of self-discipline, prompting me to complete the tasks at hand and follow the ground rules laid.

Reiterating that everything was on the budget-cutting table, the executive officers winnowed the list to the following items for further consideration under the cutback schema presented above:

- *Salary containment or reduction:* Reduce student staff in the residence halls and recreation center; eliminate graduate assistantships in parent programs, recreational services, community and volunteer services, and student activities; capture vacancy savings by continuing a soft hiring freeze except for campus police officers; reduce or eliminate summer student health services; study reducing professional staff positions to nine-month positions in career services.

- *Eliminate, redesign, or defer programs:* Redesign select-support positions giving incumbents new responsibilities; eliminate or redesign live-in coordinator positions; consider outsourcing campus scheduling; move summer orientation to the week before fall semester; expand a facilities position in the recreation center to include responsibilities in the new campus center.
- *Nonsalary containment or reduction:* Reduce annual furniture, fixtures, and equipment purchase for residence halls; reduce operating hours of the recreation center; reduce professional travel; encourage on-campus Webinars and home-grown development opportunities; replace printed parking brochures with electronic versions; and turn off the landline telephones in the residence halls except for resident assistants.
- *New revenue opportunities:* Increase the faculty and staff lunch fee in the cafeteria; explore offering alumni memberships for using the recreation center; increase all parking violations by five dollars.

A Success Story for the Division of Student Life. Most of the options have been implemented in the 2009–2010 academic year. They were offered in good faith and were well received by fellow vice presidents as meeting Student Life's fair share of our collective burden.

The following points were considered in weighing these options: the actual revenues saved and lost, the relationship to the university's vision and mission, comparisons against benchmarking data and best practices, our own assessment data, the potential impact on student engagement and development, and the impact on student recruitment and retention. The write-up of these options covered about three pages and reflected a pro-and-con format.

Significantly, two major options were not accepted, another resulted in new services being implemented for a net revenue gain, and one was creatively resolved to much satisfaction. The major options not accepted were moving the new-student summer orientation to the week before the Fall semester begins and reducing professional staff positions to nine-month positions in career services. In terms of our summer orientation, it was agreed that this was a significant yield activity for admissions and would continue unchanged in its current form. In terms of the summer health program, executive officers quickly saw that it would be counterproductive to eliminate summer health services while there was an ongoing academic initiative to increase summer school attendance. Seeing that summer health services was running at a net cost of about fifteen thousand dollars over revenue, it was decided that we would increase the summer health fee by two dollars to cover the deficit.

The major win-win solution to emerge was the continuation of the seven residential learning coordinator positions. My analysis of institutional research data demonstrated that the coordinators' presence in the halls was correlated to an increased collective grade point average for all resident students. In addition, first- and second-year resident students were being retained at higher rates than off-campus students. It also appeared that these seven professionals were helping to develop the academic success communities that reinforced the "Winthrop brand," and their presence also allowed quicker intervention with students exhibiting troubled behavior and created a seamless environment between students' in-class and out-of-class experiences. To signal the increasingly hybrid nature of their positions, we added the title of "academic associate" to their "residential learning coordinator" title. This formal link prompted us to rewrite their job descriptions and give them responsibilities for teaching the freshman seminar course (something they did without extra compensation). This yielded a salary savings in the University College payroll and provided the University College (which has no full-time dedicated faculty) with a cadre of instructors who had a student development expertise. Already these residential learning coordinators have become involved with designing extra academic counseling for premajors, assisting with planning the common book program, providing direct academic advising for new students, and assisting with new student orientation and financial aid.

These changes have been a success story for the institution, so far managing these processes well allowed the institution to progress in fulfilling its vision and mission. Significant cuts have been made throughout the university's divisions. However, the institution decided early on that cuts would not be exactly uniform in terms of their percentage reduction. The Division of Student Life benefited from this decision. If strict proportional cuts had been followed, the cuts would have been of a much different magnitude in campus life.

The state declared another allocation cutback of 9 percent just five months into the current 2009–2010 fiscal year. Fortunately the processes established had allowed a contingency fund to be established for such an eventuality. This is not to mention the elephant in the room: we have not seen any discussion on the part of state actors to figure out how to compensate through the current state tax structure for the millions our institution and others have received from the federal stabilization funds that expire on June 30, 2011.

Lessons and Conclusions

The comparative success for student affairs portrayed by this narrative was not because of any single action or attribute. There are many cumulative causal lessons that all came into play that include:

- Articulate your student affairs mission clearly and frequently, and ensure that it is closely aligned with the institution's vision and mission. This includes establishing an internal brand identity on campus for internal customers that include students, staff, and faculty.
- Hire student affairs staff who understand how their functional expertise contributes to the institution's vision and mission. They must also receive

positive reinforcement as well so they are cognizant while being constant contributors to the core values of their institution.

- Demonstrate how your student affairs staff contributes to the university's core values.
- The SSAO must establish respectful and ongoing relationships with all other executive officers. This may be fostered sometimes by asking simply, "How can my staff or I contribute to your success?" A corollary is that the student affairs staff must create relationships with faculty that help both to better understand their respective roles on campus (Ardaiolo, 1993). A more significant corollary during fiscally constrained times may be to know your president's predispositions, administrative style, and wishes for your own area of responsibility.
- Collect and disseminate relevant data and outcomes to substantiate any requests or arguments. Knowing and being able to access all such data, including budget data, are very helpful for the SSAO. It is also assumed the SSAO has a clear picture that can be articulately presented of all the activities within student affairs the data reports.

By following an executive-led budget-reduction process that is guided by values and principles, a university can continue to make progress despite budgetary setbacks. Seeing the overall budget picture through the vision, mission, and core values lens can provide a clear, far-focused vision.

References

Ardaiolo, F. P. "Ground Rules for Managing in Tough Times." *Leadership Exchange*, 2009, 7(3), 16–17.

Ardaiolo, F. P. "Involving Faculty with Student Affairs: Some Personal Pointers." *College Student Affairs Journal*, 1993, 13(1), 24–28.

Winthrop University. "University College Mission Statement." 2009. Retrieved July 9, 2009, from http://www.winthrop.edu/uc/.

Winthrop University. "Vision of Distinction, 2009–2010." 2009–2010. Retrieved December 18, 2009, from http://www.winthrop.edu/uploadedFiles/president/09–10VoD.pdf

Winthrop University. Division of Student Life. "Mission Statement." 2009. Retrieved July 9, 2009, from http://www.winthrop.edu/student-life/default.aspx.

FRANK P. ARDAIOLO is vice president for student life and associate professor at Winthrop University in Rock Hill, South Carolina.

NEW DIRECTIONS FOR STUDENT SERVICES • DOI: 10.1002/ss

7

The final chapter provides a quick and easy reference of some of this volume's most salient points.

Developing Budget Models, Communication Strategies, and Relationships to Mitigate the Pain of Tough Economic Times

Lori E. Varlotta, Barbara C. Jones, John H. Schuh

Every reader of this volume will determine which information is most relevant to his or her home campus. Like our readers, we, as editors of the book, have identified prominent overarching themes and have organized this chapter around three of them. Accordingly, we highlight the three macrolevel approaches—identifying and implementing appropriate budget models and strategies, designing and disseminating effective communications, and creating and relying on key campus relations—that should help student affairs leaders get to the other side of almost any budget crisis. We end by posing several questions that warrant additional thought and ongoing response.

Budget Strategies and Models

No matter the type of institution or the difficulty of the budget challenges at hand, a common call has sounded on campuses across the county: get ready for change because the days of business as usual are officially over. Although readying students, campus employees, and stakeholders for change is a difficult—not to mention ongoing—task, perhaps the most pragmatic and symbolic way to signal the new era is to modify both the

New Directions for Student Services, no. 129, Spring 2010 © Wiley Periodicals, Inc.
Published online in Wiley InterScience (www.interscience.wiley.com) • DOI: 10.1002/ss.353

underlying process and the campuswide models associated with routine budget cycles.

Appropriately altering the means and ends of any university budget is a sure way for senior administrators to capture attention, garner input, organize and disseminate emerging and resulting information, and create and strengthen campus relationships. Before discussing how communication and relationships can frame and fuel the times ahead, this section outlines the change in strategies and models that leaders might consider.

Changing Budget Processes. Often university leaders are loath to change (or fix) what "isn't broken." This means that many of the processes and strategies that undergird today's campus budgets are likely to be long-standing ones that have been relatively immune to revisions or modifications. While traditional strategies may have worked during routine times of gradual growth or decline, they are likely ill suited to address budget cycles that unfold in drastically declining economies. To determine if the campus's current budget process is appropriate and effective during a recession, academic leaders such as SSAOs should:

- Review the overall process in general and then scrutinize the subprocesses that constitute it. Pay special attention to who is involved when, and determine whether participants or deadlines need to change in response to the larger economic issues.
- Make process changes as necessary, and communicate them broadly.
- Rely on data. All budget processes should be data driven and rely on relevant, timely, and accurate evidence. During tough times, budget pleas are far less compelling than evidence-based proposals that show how and why the requested resources will be used.
- Hold themselves accountable for spending funds wisely and for being prudent stewards of student fees. Especially when times are tough, students and parents want to know exactly where their money is going. They also want assurance that their hard-earned money is well spent on things that matter (to them).

Changing Budget Models. While the incremental budget model is the most common one used in academe, it is the least suited to critically examine and analytically adjust previous allocations. Encouraging colleagues on the cabinet or the budget office to set aside the model they are most familiar with can be a risky and daunting task, but one that effective budget managers should consider during budget crises. Student affairs leaders can draw from the following points to help substantiate any proposal that argues against the continued use of an incremental model:

- Incremental budgeting is an automatic rather than analytical approach to budgeting. As such, it neither prompts managers to modify beyond the margins nor get to the crux of any substantive issue that needs to be addressed or reexamined when resources shrink.

- Other budget models are better equipped to analyze prior resource distribution and link allocations to planning. A single model or a combination of models may be apropos to the situation at hand.
- It may make sense for various programs to go back to the basics and determine what they are able to offer and maintain in recession-like years. In such a case, where zero-based budgeting is helpful, directors first need to identify the one, two, three, or more programs and services that they plan to offer or continue. Then they must determine how to most efficiently and effectively deliver the prioritized programs or services, costing them out from scratch, with an eye for cost savings rather than relying on what has always been done.
- No matter which model or combination of models is used, effective managers must show how budget decisions are linked to and informed by the strategic plan and university priorities. Neither should be abandoned when resources shrink.
- When engaging in budget decision making at small private schools, administrators must constantly balance enrollment assumptions and projections with endowment assumptions and projections. They must also be well versed in yields, auxiliary margins, bond rates, market indexes, and other financial concepts that are prevalent in the development of institutional budgets.

Communications

Once the decision to modify or change budget models or processes has been made, those decisions must be disseminated to the campus community—to faculty, staff, students, and other stakeholders. Accurate, timely, and relevant communication is the lifeline for all colleges and universities; it is especially critical in this current economic environment where rapidly occurring change is affecting large numbers of staff, departments, and entire campuses. The ways information is communicated play a significant part in how any forthcoming changes are interpreted, received, and acted on. Therefore, it is important for student affairs leaders to understand the role of communications, identify and work with appropriate stakeholders, effectively position student affairs, and use tools that ensure accurate and timely organization and dissemination of information.

Critical Role. Communication plays a critical role in describing and responding to the financial crisis at hand. To actualize these proactive and reactive roles, student affairs leaders should:

- Present factual, reliable information in a timely manner.
- Deliver a consistent message.

- Ensure that difficult messages are delivered in an appropriately caring and compassionate tone.
- Find the balance between full transparency and top-down decision making. In doing so, weigh the pros and cons of a fully inclusive process against those associated with a process that is executive-led and implemented.
- Use communiqués to explicitly link budget decisions to strategic initiatives.

Stakeholders. University administrators and student affairs professionals alike serve a variety of stakeholders, including students, parents, boards, staff, faculty, alumni and donors. While SSAOs and other campus leaders need to send consistent overall messages, some communications should be explicitly shaped for specific constituents. Student affairs leaders should consider the following points when communicating with their key groups:

- Have a consistent general message, but hone in on the unique needs of each group.
- Anticipate the reactions of each group, and be ready to address their individual issues.
- Involve formal and informal leaders in the organization and sharing of important information.
- Encourage input by providing various avenues (interactive Web sites, focus groups, surveys, letter campaigns) for stakeholders to share ideas or feedback.

Tools. In any university, information can be communicated in numerous ways. Administrators must keep multiple devices in their toolbox and be able to choose the appropriate ones for the job at hand. In making this decision, leaders should remember that:

- E-mail is a quick and efficient method for delivering the same message to a large number of people at the same point in time; however, e-mail must be carefully crafted to avoid being received as cold and impersonal.
- Public forums and group discussions involve people and make them feel empowered.
- Redundancy is important. Crucial statements, assumptions, and proposals should be frequently repeated to reduce confusion and prevent rumors.
- Consistent format and timing of division-head messages reduce problems that occur when one division receives information before another.

Positioning Student Affairs. While instructional activities are rightfully paramount, the programs and services of student affairs have become increasingly important in helping academic institutions fully achieve their goals. To position student affairs as a powerful partner and meaningful contributor toward meeting these goals, division leaders must communicate pertinent successes, achievements, and divisional alignments with institutional mission. Toward that end, student affairs leaders should:

- Demonstrate through data the ways student affairs helps to operationalize the institution's mission.
- Establish the role of student affairs before the crisis.
- Be a team player with other senior staff.
- Offer any reduction options that student affairs can bear, given the multiple financial structures in the division.

Relationships in the Budgeting Process

While optimally communicating budget decisions to relevant campus constituents is a high priority, the relationships that student affairs leaders create with their constituents are equally important, especially during times of budget crisis. The relationships that SSAOs build and maintain with students, staff within and beyond the division, their leadership team, and other institutional leaders play an important part in how decision making unfolds in tough budget times.

Relationships with Students. Students' tuition and fees are often the most sizable revenue that the institution receives. Therefore, it is crucial for student affairs leaders to:

- Establish ongoing relationships with students.
- Know the influential student leaders.
- Keep students apprised of budget issues, especially if fee increases are a likely option for addressing the shortfall.

Relationships with Parents. At baccalaureate institutions that primarily enroll traditional-age students, parents are particularly important since many of them cover the majority of the costs associated with their son's or daughter's education. Given parents' contribution, financial and otherwise, student affairs leaders should:

- Keep parents informed through electronic and possibly other modes of communication.
- Seek their opinions and reactions.
- Educate the parent board or council, if it exists, so that it can help communicate and support university budget decisions.

Relationships with Staff. Periodically providing staff at all levels of the organization with a picture of the division's budgetary situation is an effective way to discourage rumors and reduce unfounded speculation that can erode a healthy work environment. In drawing this picture, student affairs leaders might keep in mind that:

- Staff need to realize how budget reductions might affect them personally so that they can make appropriate and timely career decisions.
- Staff find electronic information and brief forums to be a good way of keeping them updated on time-sensitive issues such as enrollment, state budget decisions, and the termination of extramural funding sources such as grants.

Relationships with Divisional Colleagues. The relationship that student affairs leaders have with their management team is critical. To maximize the potential of this group, student affairs leaders should:

- Keep all managers informed of the division's overall budgetary situation.
- Be sure that all managers understand their own budgets and are positioned to help develop reduction or cost-saving strategies for the division.
- Understand the dynamics of the group, fully use individuals, and collect budget talent and expertise, especially during a budget crisis.
- Serve, when necessary, as a mediator between staff whose individual department goals conflict with each other or with institutional goals. An example of the former might include the conflicts that emerge between an admissions office that is trying to bring in a large class and a financial aid office that is trying to package and offer appropriate levels of aid to accepted students.

Relationships with Colleagues Outside the Division. Particularly during budget recessions, student affairs leaders must maintain good relationships with various campus colleagues, including those in the institution's budget office, the controller or treasurer's office, and academic affairs. Often people in these offices can assist SSAOs with the policies and procedures that can affect their ability to make the changes necessary to achieve budget reductions. To make sure that relationships with these key players are strong before an economic downturn begins, SSAOs should:

- Begin establishing relationships early in their tenure at the institution.
- Continually work at strengthening these relationships so that any forthcoming campuswide reductions can be discussed in an environment of trust and collegiality.

Relationships with Other Senior Leaders. When student affairs leaders have positive and productive relationships with other executive offices, difficult decisions are easier to negotiate and finalize. On highly functioning campuses, such leaders wear an institutional hat in addition to representing their units and departments, that is, they consider alternatives that serve the entire institution, not just their own units, even if that means

NEW DIRECTIONS FOR STUDENT SERVICES • DOI: 10.1002/ss

absorbing disproportional cuts in some of their own departments. To develop this macrolevel perspective, SSAOs should:

- Establish strong working relationships particularly with counterparts in academic affairs and business affairs.
- Master the art of negotiation.
- Bolster partnerships and collaborations that promote the continuation of hybrid types of services and programs.
- Understand the expectations that the president has for his or her senior staff.
- Be intimately familiar with university budget and priorities and the ways student affairs contribute to the overall university budget.

Conclusion

This chapter has highlighted three aspects of importance to senior student affairs officers: identifying and implementing appropriate budget models and strategies, designing and disseminating effective communications, and creating and relying on key campus relations. As institutions continue to engage in the challenge of managing resources in difficult financial times, student affairs must play a leadership role in this process. We must continue to hone our skills and knowledge in order to participate in the shaping of the future of higher education.

LORI E. VARLOTTA is the vice president of student affairs at California State University, Sacramento.

BARBARA C. JONES is vice president for student affairs at Miami University in Oxford, Ohio.

JOHN H. SCHUH is Distinguished Professor of Education at Iowa State University.

NEW DIRECTIONS FOR STUDENT SERVICES • DOI: 10.1002/ss

INDEX